THE ROUTLEDGE GUIDE TO INTERVIEWING

The Routledge Guide to Interviewing sets out a well-tested and practical approach and methodology: what works, difficulties and dangers to avoid and key questions which must be answered *before* you set out. Background methodological issues and arguments are considered and drawn upon but the focus is on what is ethical, legally acceptable and productive:

- Rationale (why, what for, where, how)
- Ethics and legalities (informed consent, data protection, risks, embargoes)
- Resources (organisational, technical, intellectual)
- Preparation (selecting and approaching interviewees, background and biographical research, establishing credentials, identifying topics)
- Technique (developing expertise and confidence)
- Audio-visual interviews
- Analysis (modes, methods, difficulties)
- Storage (archiving and long-term preservation)
- Sharing resources (dissemination and development).

From death row to the mansion of a head of state, small kitchens and front parlours, to legislatures and presbyteries, Anna Bryson and Seán McConville's wide interviewing experience has been condensed into this book. The material set out here has been acquired by trial, error and reflection over a period of more than four decades. The interviews have ranged from the delightfully straightforward to the painfully difficult to the near impossible – with a sprinkling of those that were impossible.

Successful interviewing draws on the survival skills of everyday life. This guide will help you to adapt, develop and apply these innate skills. Including useful information such as sample waivers, internet resources, hints and checklists, it provides sound and plain-speaking support for the oral historian, social scientist and investigator.

Anna Bryson is Research Lecturer at Queen Mary, University of London. She has considerable experience of conducting interviews for social and historical investigation. Recent publications encompass ethnographical research on Northern Ireland, prison diaries, biography and criminology. She has advised both statutory and private organisations on the design and implementation of complex interview-based projects.

Seán McConville is Professor of Law and Public Policy at Queen Mary, University of London. He has researched and taught at leading universities on both sides of the Atlantic. His interests and publications range widely, from Islamic criminal law to prison architecture, but have clustered around the philosophy and administration of punishment – historically, comparatively and in current debates. His publications include *Irish Political Prisoners 1848–1922* (Routledge, 2003) and *Irish Political Prisoners 1920–1962* (Routledge, 2013).

'Bryson and McConville have produced a comprehensive survival guide for new and seasoned interviewers which takes our everyday experience of social interaction as a starting point for demystifying the interview process. Covering all the bases from initial approaches to potential interviewees to storage and management, this book is a comprehensive "how to" guide that should help to minimise mistakes and maximise the value of the interview process. Designed for a wide readership, from academics to community workers, therapists to artists, this is a plain speaking troubleshooting guide to the world of the interview.'

Lynn Abrams, *University of Glasgow, UK*

THE ROUTLEDGE GUIDE TO INTERVIEWING

Oral history, social enquiry and investigation

Anna Bryson and Seán McConville
assisted by Mairead McClean

Routledge
Taylor & Francis Group

LONDON AND NEW YORK

First published 2014
by Routledge
2 Park Square, Milton Park, Abingdon, Oxon OX14 4RN

and by Routledge
711 Third Avenue, New York, NY 10017

Routledge is an imprint of the Taylor & Francis Group, an informa business

British Library Cataloguing in Publication Data
A catalogue record for this book is available from the British Library

Library of Congress Cataloging in Publication Data
Bryson, Anna.
The Routledge Guide to Interviewing : Oral History, Social Enquiry and
Investigation / By Anna Bryson and Seán McConville.
pages cm
1. Oral history–Handbooks, manuals, etc. 2. Interviewing–Handbooks,
manuals, etc. I. McConville, Seán. II. Title.
D16.14.B79 2013
907.2–dc23
2013017261

ISBN: 978-0-415-71074-9 (hbk)
ISBN: 978-0-415-71075-6 (pbk)
ISBN: 978-1-315-88223-9 (ebk)

Typeset in Bembo Std
by Saxon Graphics Ltd, Derby

Printed and bound in Great Britain by
TJ International Ltd, Padstow, Cornwall

CONTENTS

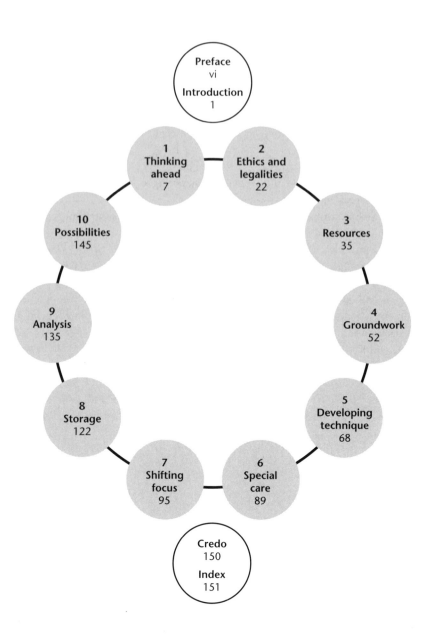

PREFACE

Throughout this book, in order to protect the confidence of interviewees, names and casual details in some illustrative examples have been changed. All are products of actual encounters.

We invited a number of colleagues and interviewees to contribute spotlight pieces. Our thanks to the following: Graham Baré, Eamonn Boyce, Mark Christal, Leah Foley, Tony Hickey, Caitriona Kelly, Sarah Lorimer, Laurence McKeown and Larry Moley. Mairead McClean provided an extended piece on audio-visual interviews. Linda Ballard and Peter Carson of the Ulster Folk and Transport Museum offered valuable insights into curation and the use of audio equipment; Conor McCarthy gave IT advice and Barbara Mohan introduced us to the fashion industry.

Maureen Kelly of Keystone Law kindly reviewed the references to the law in this publication. This was based upon the law of England and Wales and is for reference only. It does not constitute legal advice and should not be relied upon as such. Specific legal advice relevant to your jurisdiction and your specific circumstances must be sought separately before taking any action based on this publication.

INTRODUCTION

Interviews are essentially verbal transactions in a wide variety of settings. They go on all the time, but we hardly ever recognise them. What happens? What skills are at work? How can they be adapted and developed?

Daily encounters

6.30am

Get up. Lift the baby. Get a bottle of milk. Change and dress him. Get dressed before he finishes it. Waken the toddler and take her to the toilet. Get her a drink and quickly prepare the breakfast. Deal with the toddler's tantrum and negotiate what she will eat. Feed the baby while the toddler is eating. Dress the toddler. Eat your own breakfast, get washed and dressed, pack up for crèche and work. Go back to collect your wallet.

Although they don't generally have time to think about it, parents routinely employ skills that are key to effective interviewing. These include preparation, anticipation, concentration, intuition, flexibility, patience, active listening and communication.

8.15am

Arrive at crèche. Meet other parents and childcare workers.

Again, without thinking about it, you practise interviewing skills in the course of daily encounters with peers and professionals. When a parent suggests a play-date in the hall of the crèche you quickly read them for clues. Depending on their intonation and body language you might wonder if they have been press-ganged into the proposal by their child (or yours). Before responding you will quickly make an assessment of them based on how they look and sound, their eye contact, their general demeanour. You will simultaneously read the reaction of third parties such as an onlooking childcare worker. You may be forced into bluffing as you grasp to remember their child's name. At the same time you are taking off coats and hats, dealing with unexpected emotional outbursts, preparing to hand over completed paperwork, and keeping an eye on your watch. This is in many ways similar to the first few minutes of an interview as you engage with the interviewee and their relatives, set up your machinery, attend to important documentation, and subtly pay attention to the clock.

8.45am

Arrive at work. Meet colleagues.

Whether you are a lorry-driver, a cleaner, a teacher, an office junior, a manager, a forestry worker, a healthcare professional or a joiner, you will throughout your working day conduct interviews of one kind or another (with customers, clients or colleagues). You will encounter all kinds of people: those who are cooperative, friendly, cold, aggressive, talkative, distracting, angry, helpful or kind. Some of these you can prepare for; most take their place in the daily round.

12.30pm

Meet a friend for lunch.

What does it say about you if you are late? Are you conscious of how you look? To what extent does the location influence your ability to engage in relaxed conversation? Is there a lot of background noise? Are you distracted by the unwanted intervention of a third party? How does this make you feel? Before we begin to talk, we communicate. How do you greet your friend? How do they look? Are they happy to see you? What is their reaction? Are they distracted, upset, unwell, feeling positive, at ease, delighted to see you? Almost subconsciously you have prepared for this meeting. You will most likely think about the last time you met or spoke, what is going on in their lives, and you will want to show interest, respect and care by asking about these things. You will listen intently to what they have to say. Depending on your own mood, you might want to rant about the day's proceedings, to get off your chest the things that are bothering you – whether at work or at home.

The Daily Round

In a given week you will engage in a multitude of interviews. Encounters with family members, friends, social welfare officers, professionals (nurses, doctors, dentists, physiotherapists and so on), sales assistants, telecommunications staff, law enforcement officers, fitness instructors, hairdressers, butchers, postmasters, car salesmen, estate agents and mechanics – all these test and develop your communication skills.

The minute you walk through the door of a shop the sales assistant is making an assessment and processing a range of questions. Are you likely to steal? What is your style? Is it worth investing time in you? How much money are you likely to have and spend? In an instant a car dealer will ascertain how much or how little you know – makes, models, pitfalls – and whether you are a potential buyer or a 'tyre-kicker'. While attending to your needs they will engage in 'small-talk' as they try to establish some kind of a rapport. You in turn are forming an assessment: how genuine and interested are they? Can you trust their judgement?

In your everyday life you read clues, assess risk, seek assurances, conduct background research, provide sureties and communicate effectively. These are survival skills: you are already well on your way to being an experienced and effective interviewer.

This manual will help you to adapt, develop and apply these skills. It is intended as a practical guide to interviewing for a wide range of purposes and in a variety of settings. Together we draw on experience going back forty-five years. Our interviews have ranged widely – from prisons and courts, Parliament buildings and the Office of the President, to small kitchens and street corners. Interviewees include death row and natural life prisoners, homemakers, paramilitaries, athletes, priests and other clergy, archbishops, victims, former premiers and a variety of ministers. We have conducted these interviews in a range of contexts: parole applications, litigation, appraisals, university admissions, sentencing decisions, family proceedings and academic research – social, legal and historical. Sharing our experience, we have designed and delivered interview training sessions covering interview integrity procedures, processing and storing, styles and techniques, technical matters and the necessary legal, ethical and professional standards. Our trainees have developed their own interview-based projects and we are very gratified to have trained trainers.

There is an enormous appetite for interview-based research, stimulated by the astonishing growth in local, family and community history. But as we assembled training materials and reflected upon and sought to use our varied experiences, the need for a manual such as this presented itself again and again. Some of our training participants were seasoned interviewers, but they too required a systematic overview of the methodology and an up-to-date practical guide in order to continue their work with confidence.

There is an ever more manifest need and mounting political pressure to address residual legacy and memory issues in post-conflict areas such as Northern Ireland and the Balkans. This must be balanced by considerations of legal and ethical probity and conservative and prudential operation. Scandals over the leakage of interview recordings have underlined the need to understand legal and moral obligations. In close-knit and delicately balanced communities, thoughtlessness – and even a momentary failure to think ahead – can mean that this type of work does more harm than good. Ill-conducted work is not just a waste; it is retrograde, distresses (could even endanger), and it breeds cynicism and resentment: above all, none of us wants to feel used. Civic responsibility, as well as teaching and research ethics, demand that researchers learn to look beyond interviews and all that surrounds them and to anticipate consequences. As decent citizens, our approach must be as far as possible from those who 'parachute in' and then move on regardless.

Given the fractured past state of many post-conflict communities and what in many cases remains a precarious equilibrium, research must be justified and conducted with sympathy, impartiality and scrupulousness, always taking care to provide a context and to seek out narratives and experiences that span the entire community. Interviewing in circumstances of considerable tension (for example, in the aftermath of prison riots in the United States), we knew that a false step could have aggravated the situation in most undesirable ways. Discretion and good judgement are paramount: to achieve those and match them to the circumstances can be a formidable challenge. The consequences may seem less cataclysmic, but the ripples of poorly conceived, badly-prepared or ill-judged interviews in a workplace, locality or interest group will almost certainly have long-lasting and regrettable effects.

This manual sets out a tested and practical methodology, together with an overview of key legal and ethical issues. It is designed with both a general and an academic readership in mind. Our trainees have ranged from graduate students at leading universities to those who have had limited formal education (but no shortage of common sense, ability and energy). It is our hope that the skills which this book aims to develop are flexible and adaptable to a wide range of purposes. We present it in the nature of an all-terrain vehicle – as suitable for those exploring extreme social tension as for a researcher working in a positive and supportive setting.

The interview lies close to the most humane of our values – respect for others and an unremitting attempt to understand each other, and through that, ourselves. The unexamined life is scarcely worth living because it fails to exercise our most defining human ability: consciousness transformed by reflection. And, reflection – which we do alone – must always involve others. They are as much a condition of our existence as air and water. The interview is but a part of the constant interaction, mental and social, that lays down the stuff of which we are made. There are bad interviews and there are bad and ill-motivated interviewers, no doubt, but there are in the body of techniques on which we draw and which we set out here, some attractive and glorious possibilities.

As in most fields of knowledge and skill there are volumes of small print. There are also schools, classes and even desks and lone stools of thought – sometimes fierce and prescriptive, deriving from strongly and (generally) honestly-held views. We do not dismiss these but have turned our gaze more to the practical and ordered our thoughts and preferences along the via media, the path that can be trod. It is not that those points of contending orthodoxy are unimportant – they can be illuminating and instructive – but they need to be explored in other settings.

Emerging from infancy and childhood we learn that we are not the centre of the world. We acquire the skills of self-effacement, balance in conversation and the expression of interest in others. But underneath it all, the infant lurks, waiting for the opportunity to command attention. There are exceptions, but most people have a desire to talk, to relate experiences, views and hopes; to reveal. The stage can be made available, expectations agreed, and encouragement provided. When all this is well and sensitively done there can be an act of creation. Check your equipment one last time, give all your attention to your subject: let the interview begin!

Anna Bryson
Seán McConville
Queen Mary, University of London
April 2013

1

THINKING AHEAD

Why am I here?

There are many questions to ask yourself before embarking on an interview. The first is:

- Why do I want to conduct an interview or a series of interviews?

  The answer might include one or more of the following:

- I am interested in preserving family and local history and I want to elicit information and insights from elderly relatives and friends before they die.
- I am conducting historical research and I want to check and supplement official records.
- There are gaps in the documentary archives that can only be closed (however imperfectly) by interviews.
- My interviews will focus on those who are underrepresented in available source material (for example, women, young people, ethnic and religious minorities, illiterates) and thus help to create a more democratic version of history.
- My research will be humanised by including the perspective of individuals who lived through the period or events under investigation.
- My prose needs the lift of telling anecdotes.
- I am a journalist for whom interviews are a staple source of information.
- I am interested in the way in which people remember and I want to collect narratives for analysis (feminist, genre, post-colonial, literary etc.).
- I am interested in the history and mechanics of language and I want to record, preserve and examine a range of dialects.

- I am a folklorist and I wish to capture the oral tradition of a particular area, community or locale.
- I am an anthropologist interested in social patterns, practices and adaptations across a range of cultures.
- I work with the elderly and I want to record interviews as reminiscence therapy.
- I am involved in peace and reconciliation work and I see interviews as a healing mechanism – an opportunity for survivors to put on record their version of a bitterly contested past.
- I am a novelist/playwright/film maker and I wish to collect stories for literary adaptation.

As we have noted, interviews – and the skills necessary to conduct them – are relevant to a vast array of vocational and everyday life activities.

These include:

- Exchanges with social workers, probation officers, social welfare officials, community and youth leaders
- Job interviews (including via Skype)
- Market research
- Consumer feedback (customers, patients, clients, students)
- Performance appraisals
- Disciplinary assessments and investigations
- Medical consultation (encounters with doctors, nurses, psychologists, counsellors and other professionals)
- Interrogation of witnesses in the course of criminal investigations
- Solicitation of information for tribunals or committees of enquiry
- Social encounters
    - Meeting friends
    - Courting potential partners
    - Online dating
    - Speed dating.

CORPORATE INTERVIEWS

As the manager of a Human Resource department in a large multi-national organisation, I have direct experience of the importance of the interview process. We have responsibility for engaging with staff on a wide range of issues. The extent of HR engagement and the level of formality will depend on the size and culture of the organisation. For most HR functions, however, the interview process remains a core tool. It is used to deal with disciplinary, grievance and performance-related matters. In this short piece I want to highlight some of the key skills and factors in play in recruitment.

The ultimate aim in recruitment is to fill the vacant post with the most suitable candidate. The interview process must be structured in such a way that it enables the panel to assess candidates in an objective and transparent manner. Preparation is the key to avoiding unproductive or inappropriate questions (which may run contrary to employment or equality legislation and guidelines) and to reducing tension for both candidates and interviewers. Attention to detail can impact greatly on the success of the process. The location for the interview sets the tone. It is very important that the setting is comfortable for all concerned. Simple things matter. The room should be of an appropriate size to cater for the total number of people attending the interview (people should be able to sit comfortably, not too close but not so far apart that they need to raise their voices to communicate). Conducting an interview in sub-zero temperatures or in extreme heat can make the experience very uncomfortable. It also important to have water or other refreshments available, but a word of caution – nerves can lead to shaky hands! Pour the water in advance; watching an interviewee struggling with a tightly fitted lid and then witnessing them pour water all over themselves makes for all-round embarrassment.

The first requirement for an interviewer on a recruitment panel is to understand the brief. They must examine the role that is being filled and review the key tasks and competencies required. There are few more cringeworthy moments than witnessing an interviewer ask a question that betrays that he or she either does not understand the nature of the job to be filled or has not taken the time to read the documents submitted by the candidate. (Bear in mind that an interview is a two-way process. In addition to answering questions, the interviewee is making an assessment of the nature of the employer (as represented by the panel), and the wisdom of accepting the post if offered.)

Fair and transparent comparison of candidates calls for structured and consistent questioning. This does not necessarily mean slavish adherence to a schedule. A skilled interviewer will balance the requirement to cover key requirements while listening closely to the answers provided by the candidates. He or she will use follow-up questions to move the candidate in a seamless manner through the competencies. Getting this balance right, judging when to re-direct or politely interrupt a candidate to bring them back on track, can make a significant difference to the performance of the applicant and the overall quality of the interview.

In recent years the use of technology has become more prevalent. Often a panel member will join the discussion by conference call. More and more interviews are now being conducted through audio visual facilities similar to

Skype. The benefits and savings are obvious, and experience indicates that if the technology is of a good standard, and the interviewers are well prepared, the process can run smoothly. However, the technology is critically important; check and recheck before engaging in a live interview. If there is a time lag this can lead to a degree of disengagement on the part of the panel. All interviewers must prepare to give total concentration to remote candidates, whether or not eye contact is possible. In my opinion the restriction of the camera is not necessarily a disadvantage, because I feel that too much can be read into body language; it can be telling, but it does not necessarily communicate how a candidate will perform in the advertised role. The most effective interviews focus on the key skills required for the jobs and elicit clear information on the experience and capability of the applicants. A time lag does undoubtedly make it more difficult to interject with impromptu questions; the panel must rehearse in advance the fine detail of their questioning strategy.

The interview process remains a vital element of selection, performance, grievance and competency appraisal for employers. It typically takes its place alongside other tools such as personality profiles and 360-degree feedback (whereby a staff member will get feedback on a range of competencies from subordinates, peers and managers). In my experience, successful interviews demand careful preparation and planning, strict attention to detail, flexibility, intuition, and skilful questioning. The stakes are high: get it right and you will recruit, nurture and promote the right personnel, with all the attendant benefits for your organisation; get it wrong and the costs can prove hard to limit.

Where do I want to go?

It is important to consider at the outset the final destination of the information that you collect. Interviewees will naturally want to know what will become of their account and they cannot give informed consent until they know what you intend to do with the material.

Outputs might include:

- Archive collection (open/restricted)
- Print publication (article, book, report)
- Exhibition (local library or archive, museum, online)
- Documentary (radio, film, online)
- Literary adaptation (film, play, novel, short story, comic strip etc.)
- Website (or contribution to an existing online forum)
- Staff records
- Official report.

An obvious challenge is that it is difficult when starting out to anticipate all potential uses of the material.

There is also a common dilemma: pitch too broadly and your interviewees may become uneasy at the level of potential exposure; pitch too narrowly and you close off possibilities that may arise as the work develops. This dilemma can only be resolved in a frank and open consultation with the interviewee.

It may be possible to revisit and, if necessary, revise terms and conditions when the project is more fully established, but the more thought that you give to these issues at the outset, the better.

What are the benefits?

At the beginning of this section we considered interviews as a means to an end – a way of informing a specific research output. Before considering risks and responsibilities it is worth reflecting on benefits.

We often ask trainees to reflect on what has attracted them to this type of work. Their responses include the following:

"Listening and interviewing skills are very transferable and will definitely assist me in all aspects of my work within the community."

"This training will help my organisation to tell its story and to tackle negative perceptions of it."

"What most interests me about this type of work is the range of emotions. This really helps to illustrate the impact that historical events have had on ordinary people and how they personally experience them. I think that interviews can bring a period of history to life in a way that no book can, which is very powerful."

"I will apply these skills to my research into the issue of justice in post-conflict societies."

"I want to record my community's experiences in a manner that ordinary people can relate to."

"I want to take a fresh look at historical evidence – to get beyond the photograph and letter and think about the person and life behind it."

"I'm taking more of an interest in listening to older members of my own family and community and want to find out more before it's too late."

One of the most compelling attractions of the interview method is its focus on individual experience. It forces us to confront the varied, multi-layered, sometimes muddled, and often contradictory perceptions, recollections and motives of all kinds of people. A victim may be paralysed with grief when talking about the trauma that they have endured, but remarkably composed when describing their passion for greyhound racing. A convicted murderer might be a loving mother for whom homicide formed part of an almost parallel existence. The point is not to palliate the crime in any way, but simply to acknowledge that people are capable of maintaining several different identities. In the most austere and grim prison conflicts, we have recorded instances of human kindness, toleration and humour, the memory of which has persisted for fifty years and more. Cast in so many shades of grey, oral testimonies defy neat generalisations and offer a level of detail, humanity, colour and atmosphere that is difficult to draw from other sources.

Another significant advantage is the fact that you are not confined to the annals of history: as the interviewer, you decide what you want to investigate, and can go forth and capture. As an active participant in the process, you can also challenge and refine that information as it is being collected. There is no end to the possibilities for research. In towns, villages and cities you will find exhibitions featuring interviews with all kinds of people. In the final section of this book we explore further the possibilities for dissemination of your material.

What are the risks?

Interviewing is not hazard-free and it is thus important to consider some of the risks and responsibilities that you are about to assume.

In this section we consider in turn the risks for the interviewee, for third parties and for the interviewer.

1. The interviewee

Before approaching an interviewee it is essential to put yourself in their shoes and to consider the questions that he or she almost certainly has in mind.

These include:

- Who are you?
- Why should I trust you?
- What do you want to know?
- Why?
- What for?
- Will you accurately represent me?
- Who else will see my interview account (while the interview is in process and after it is completed)?
- Who else has agreed to participate?

- What are the risks?
- What assurances can you offer?

Having established the facts, interviewees will consider a number of issues.

Investment of time

To have any hope of convincing an interviewee to take part in an interview, you must first be certain that this is a worthwhile investment of your own time. You must believe intrinsically in the value of the project, and you must be prepared to impress your interviewee with a generous measure of that same enthusiasm.

If you cannot demonstrate that you are a credible and serious person, that you are in possession of the obvious and necessary facts and that you have the resources necessary to complete your project, your request may not even be considered.

Planning is vital if you are to honour your completion obligations. Many worthy projects have failed to complete due to shortfalls in funding, most commonly at the transcription stage. If interviewees are let down at any stage in proceedings – receipt of original transcript, receipt of final edited script, or delivery of the promised outputs – they may well conclude that the exercise was a waste of their time and resolve never to participate in an interview-based project again. If they have made a significant emotional investment they may even feel exploited. This muddies the pitch for other researchers and breeds cynicism and resentment. They may also choose to complain to your sponsoring institution.

Exposure of interviewee

It is easy to underestimate just how intimidating the prospect of an interview can be. For some, the very receipt of a formal approach letter can be unsettling.

AFTERSHOCK

On the firm recommendation of one of our interviewees (and an assurance that the lady in question would be happy to contribute an interview) we issued a letter on the usual university letterhead. This set out all the relevant information about us, our sponsors, and the project.

The following week we had a call from a very angry young woman. It transpired that receipt of this letter had greatly upset her mother. By alluding to Mrs Ryans' earlier experience of imprisonment, we had reawakened a host of painful memories that had long since been consigned to the past. Unbeknown to us, prison life was on a memory chain that extended to the murder of loved ones.

Thankfully, Mrs Ryans agreed to let us visit and apologise in person. She graciously accepted our rationale and regret, and subsequently contributed to the project off the record. This was nonetheless a salutary reminder of the effect that the simple receipt of a letter can have on some interviewees, and the fact that we are often sailing in uncharted waters.

Convincing shy and reluctant interviewees to partake in a project is a time-consuming business. You need to develop a sure feel for the point at which fair and appropriate persuasion begins to feel like harassment. Make your plea, state your case, and then give the individual concerned some time to consider. If they are central to your project, you might ask a sponsor to intervene on your behalf. But if the individual does not wish to participate you must respect their wishes. If necessary you can always revisit them at a later date when the work is more fully developed (and you have more credentials to offer). In our experience it sometimes happens that an interviewee will emphatically decline, only to re-establish contact at a later date and volunteer an interview – whether due to a shift in personal or professional circumstances, or a simple change of heart. There is naturally a greater chance of this occurring if the initial encounter concluded professionally and respectfully.

It is advisable to follow up with a phone call, especially if you suspect that your witness might be unnerved by the receipt of a formal letter. It is much easier to establish rapport and good relations either in person or on the telephone, and to reassure the interviewee as to your approachability and friendliness.

Sense of inadequacy

Among the most common responses to an invitation to interview are: 'But what could I possibly have to contribute?' 'How would my experiences be relevant?' 'I was never one for books and learning,' and therefore 'You would be much better off talking to…' Frustratingly, these responses are often associated with the individuals that you most want to interview. In the next section we discuss various strategies for approaching interviewees. Throughout the interview process, reluctant witnesses need gentle reassurance that their story is worth recording. This can be achieved by a simple nod of the head, constant eye contact, and a general demeanour that communicates interest and appreciation. In some cases you will need to go further and explain why you feel that their experience or that of their community (locale, industry, vocation) should be preserved.

Reputational damage (Personal and/or Professional)

Interviewees may worry that a comment made in the course of an interview – about themselves or a third party – could cause embarrassment or damage their personal or professional life. This anxiety can increase if the individual holds a position of responsibility in the community (as a teacher, carer, employer or youth worker). (In political circles this can work in reverse: rank and file members are often concerned lest they say something that might upset the 'leadership'.)

Misrepresentation

This is a central concern. While deliberate misrepresentation has no place in an ethical interview process, misunderstandings can easily arise. The process of editing, however lightly, involves judgement and prioritisation, and as we discuss in Section 9, even simple grammatical correction can alter meaning.

The extent to which interviewees are involved in the editing process depends on the agreement that you reach at the outset, but they should, at the very least, be afforded an opportunity to review what they have said and to decide, on reflection, the extent to which their account can be made public. An extended interview is about measured reflection. You are inviting respondents to engage in a serious and honest reflection about some aspect of their life experience, and it is your duty to establish the safeguards and protocols necessary to enable and protect this process.

Re-traumatisation

Re-traumatisation is likely only to arise in a very select number of projects concerning highly emotive subjects such as physical and sexual violence, bereavement, physical or emotional abuse, abortion, employment or public-service grievance, or mental health. It is nevertheless important to be aware that in delving into someone's past we are doing just that: there can be live wires and trip switches in the most innocent-looking places. A discussion about a football match, a trip to a certain village or a specific aspect of working life can in an instant trigger a memory of a tragedy or a trauma. In most cases this is the cause of temporary upset, a passing tear, and may require nothing more than a compassionate pause in proceedings. In more extreme cases it will provoke painful and distressing memories. Safeguards against this (and indeed consideration of the wisdom of such a venture) are developed more fully in Section 6. The important thing to remember is that you are not offering a counselling service and that you must always avoid doing more harm than good.

THE COUNSELLOR'S CHAIR

Every discipline has its own methods and criteria for collecting and analysing data. My work has been mainly in a trauma and crisis setting (Rwandese genocide, refugees from Burundi and the Congo, victims of ethnic violence in Kenya, Vietnam and Gulf War veterans).

In the immediate aftermath of an atrocity, government agencies and others arrive to collect information to support a crisis-management plan. A counsellor will also record data – but from a different perspective and for different purposes. Our focus is not the statistical fact, but rather the impact of the experience on the individual.

My clients are particularly vulnerable: trust does not come easily. My primary task is to create a safe and secure atmosphere. My second is to convince them (by sustained and active listening) that I am trying to understand their pain. The very fact of talking to someone who cares is usually the beginning of a slow healing process.

Many of the skills and attributes that I employ are similar to those employed in a research setting. They include:

- Data taking
- Active listening
- Empathy
- Exploratory questioning
- Intense sensitivity to language and to the impact of my questions
- Patience
- Flexibility
- Offering feedback
- Monitoring progress
- Self-awareness (how the process is affecting me).

In contrast to interviews in a research setting I see my clients for a minimum of ten sessions over an extended period, usually months. This gives time for deep trust to develop. My approach is holistic. When the client is ready I gently introduce structure, but the pace and scope of the interview are dictated by them.

My objective is also quite different. I help my clients to process and rationalise painful memories and experiences. In my experience complete healing never takes place as the trauma scars are too deep, but counselling can help a traumatised individual to develop coping skills. This is highly skilled work: an experienced counsellor will draw on a range of approaches to best meet the needs of the individual client.

Some of my clients have given interviews for data taking or research purposes. For the most part this has not added to their pain (and in some instances it was clearly part of a healing process). It is important to note, however, that these individuals had already engaged in extensive post-traumatic counselling. Unless such a service can be offered as part of the research exercise, I would caution against inviting a traumatised person to take part in a research interview.

My concern is as much for the interviewer as for the interviewee. As professional counsellors we benefit from a highly developed support system. We have been trained to be sensitive to our own threshold for processing horrific stories, and this enables us to be present to our clients in a professional and ethically responsible manner. Without the benefit of such training and support, researchers run the risk of burn out. Trauma is not always self-evident. My advice for researchers setting out is to reflect on their own vulnerability and that of their interviewees, and to consider and respect the boundaries between clinical counselling and ethical research.

If you plan to talk to bereaved or damaged witnesses, consider the possible after-effects before approaching them. You might begin by approaching a representative organisation and asking them to talk you through particular sensitivities and risks. For example, it is possible that, as a result of revisiting painful memories, some interviewees may (unexpectedly) require professional help. This involves quite a delicate exercise of judgement. It is not for the interviewer to decide if and when an individual might benefit from a counselling service, and a suggestion to this effect might well give offence. Therefore, it is much better to establish a policy at the outset and uniformly enforce it. For example, you might want to include a standard clause in all of your introductory letters noting that the issues raised may unintentionally upset some participants, and you are therefore enclosing details of a range of counselling services in their area. Alternatively, this could be posted on your project website.

INTERVIEWING VICTIMS

I have conducted dozens of interviews in the course of both my studies and my working life. A few weeks ago I conducted my first interview with someone who had suffered a traumatic bereavement. I prepared for the interview by reading up on Tony's story, his campaign to raise awareness of victims' needs, and the background to the bereavement itself. I also consulted with a victims' rights organisation. We agreed that it was more important than ever to allow the interviewee to select the location for the interview, that I should allow plenty of time for the interview, and that I should assure the interviewee that he should feel free to take a break at any point. We also thought it important to advise Tony that he should feel free to contact me at any point after the interview. I also reassured him that if he changed his mind at any point about the inclusion of the interview in our archive we would, of course, respect his wishes.

In spite of my preparation, the actual encounter was a lot more emotional than I had anticipated. Normally I try to show empathy and understanding by focusing intently on the interviewee and maintaining eye contact. On this occasion my interviewee clearly preferred to turn away from me, facing the window and focusing on the ground. I quickly realised that this was a coping strategy which he adopted when recalling traumatic events. I felt that it was more important than ever to listen intently and to let the interviewee dictate the pace. Thankfully I had not scheduled any further appointments that day. After the interview we travelled together to a memorial garden. I felt that it was very important to spend this additional time with Tony, to show respect for his loved one, and to help him to 'come down' by talking about issues and events unrelated to the interview. It would have been wholly inappropriate for me to rush off straight after the interview.

This encounter had quite a profound effect on me. I found that it was quite a challenge to suppress my own emotions, because – quite unexpectedly – the interview evoked personal emotions and memories relating to the loss of a member of my own family. When we parted, I found myself travelling to another memorial site to reflect on my feelings. I also spoke at length to a colleague, which I found very helpful. I am nonetheless grateful for the opportunity to record this interview, and in spite of the pain, I know that Tony very much wanted to put his story on record.

2. Third parties

When you set out to interview you bear responsibility (directly or indirectly) for the reputation of institutions (for example, local history societies, trades unions, sporting organisations, schools, youth groups, third level institutes, private sector bodies and so on) to whom you are affiliated and under whose colours you sail. For those who are unaffiliated, you will almost certainly come with a recommendation from family, neighbours or friends (however distant) and to whom you will feel responsible.

You also have obligations to your interviewee. These individuals have been kind enough to gift you with their time and hospitality, and to invite you into what is often a very private sphere of their life. This brings with it a sense of duty and care that goes well beyond written assurances.

In delicately balanced and close-knit communities interviewees will often fret that something they say will upset family, neighbourly, or community relations; these situations can be drum skin tight. It is indeed difficult to discuss past events without specific reference to third parties (family members, neighbours, friends, colleagues, public figures). If it seems likely that the immediate outing of your interview material will do more harm than good, you should consider putting in place some or all of the security measures outlined in Section 6. At the very least, you will need to persuade your interviewees that you are a trustworthy person of mature discretion who will treat as confidential any potentially embarrassing or hurtful anecdotes that they choose to share with you.

We have noted that most interviewees welcome an opportunity to review and reflect on their contribution before it is made public. The most straightforward (if costly and time-consuming) way of attending to this is by agreeing to return a transcript. This enables the interviewee to make corrections, redactions or additions as they wish. With the widespread availability of sound editing software, it is now increasingly commonplace to offer the facility to edit the original recording. As we discuss in Section 9, scholars are generally opposed to any violation of the recording, citing the sanctity of the original source and the myriad ways in which future researchers may value the material. However, if you do not have the facilities and resources to offer a meaningful embargo, this may be a necessary evil.

3. The interviewer

You have a vested interest in minimising the risk of damage for your interviewees and third parties – your reputation and that of your sponsor is at stake. At the same time you must look after yourself. Interviewing is frequently an emotionally intense and draining activity. The interviewer has primary responsibility for the success of the exercise, and must pay close attention to matters both practical and interpersonal. Our interviews have typically been in the one-to-two hour range, and bearing in mind the emotional after-effects of an intense interview, it is generally unwise to schedule more than two, or at most three, appointments in any given day. Fatigue is not conducive to successful interviewing, and when combined with travel, it may well be hazardous.

Interviewees, as we know, will consider whether the encounter is likely to represent a productive use of their time. Equally, there may be occasions when you decide to walk away. This may be because your interviewee is hopelessly incoherent, or because they are angry and intent on using the opportunity to settle an old score. Processing interviews is extraordinarily time-consuming (and can be costly), and you need frequently to refer to your budget and time-scale to ensure that you are making judicious use both of your time and that of your interviewees. Withdrawing an invitation to interview must always be handled sensitively and diplomatically, taking care not to give offence.

Exposure of interviewer

When assessing risk it is important to acknowledge that an interview is an exposure both for you and the interviewee. The interviewee will want to know a little bit about your background and views, and may press you further in the course of the interview. You will be conscious of how you sound and appear, and what the interviewee's assessment of you might be. As we noted in the

Introduction, this is in many ways the stuff of everyday conversation: in almost every social encounter we are both consciously and unconsciously reading one another for hints of approval, disapproval and possible offence. Inevitably we also tend to see each other in social categories – as a farmer, a student, an elderly woman, a bank manager, a housewife; as black, white, young, old, male, female, educated, uneducated, and so on. We each bring to the interview a 'tale' – on the one hand an explanation and rationale for setting up the research project, and on the other a profile that suggested eligibility for interview.

It is important to strike the right balance between giving an open account of yourself and maintaining a degree of professional detachment. In short, the balance of enquiry should tilt firmly in the direction of the interviewee.

Personal safety

In the next section we elaborate on safeguards. Chief among these is the fact that you must not record information about crimes that have not been processed and fully determined in the appropriate criminal justice system and courts. This runs the risk, in the worst case scenario, of compromising the safety of your interviewee, named individuals, and possibly also yourself. Threats to personal safety could also arise due to careless storage of files containing individuals' contact details. Should there be a serious failure on your part, civil and criminal liability may arise. We will return to some of these issues in the context of data protection legislation.

If you are working in or out of an institution or organisation, issues of health and safety, while not absent, tend to be few. This is not to say that field research is risk-free. Travelling to see potential witnesses in their homes or workplaces and on their terms is often essential. It demonstrates that you are prepared to invest time and energy in trying to understand their perspective and that of their community and thus helps to build trust and rapport. On occasion this led us to take disproportionate risks, including impromptu meetings in the proverbial smoke-filled back rooms and accepting lone lifts with strangers. In the aftermath of one particularly hair-raising encounter we established simple safety guidelines. These include protocols such as:

- Forewarn colleagues if you plan to interview out of hours in your office.
- Always let someone else know who you are planning to meet or interview, when and where you are meeting them (and if possible leave a contact number).
- Carry appropriate ID and spare cash.
- Think carefully before agreeing to meet or interview someone about whom you know very little and for whom you do not have a direct recommendation (if in any doubt whatsoever, bring a friend to help assess the situation).
- Consider transport arrangements. Is it safe to park your car? Can you access reliable public transport? Are reputable taxi firms available?

- If you have any concerns about the suitability of the interview or meeting venue, explore and assess in advance. If necessary, suggest an alternative.
- Consider local tensions (cultural, religious and racial) and dress inconspicuously and non-provocatively.
- Keep audio equipment, laptops, cameras, smartphones and maps out of sight.
- Never interview a minor or a vulnerable person on your own.
- Never proceed to interview someone who is under the influence of alcohol or drugs.
- Debrief after each interview and report any health/safety issues. Adapt your procedures accordingly.

2

ETHICS AND LEGALITIES

We have emphasised that it is possible to do more harm than good. A sound ethical framework is thus essential.

In the spirit of the Hippocratic Oath, you should:

- at the very minimum, do no harm
- treat without exception and with equal respect all those with whom you deal
- abstain from whatever is harmful or mischievous
- protect all confidences.

Your organisation may already have a guide to good practice in research or a code of conduct which encompasses interviewing. It may also be obligatory (and it is certainly advisable) to submit your project plan and protocols to an ethics committee. If you do not have recourse to such a body, consider consulting a relevant support agency (for example, a victims' organisation) or a representative body such as a trades union.

The following sample covers most of the key issues.

Ethical principles

Equality, inclusivity & respect

- Our reach across communities, religious, ethnic, and political groups will be comprehensive and inclusive.
- We conduct our interviews with compassion, respecting the diverse needs of all participants, regardless of religious, social, cultural, ethnic or political background.

Transparency & accountability

- Our processes, procedures, funding and motivations will be accessible to all those who are participating and involved in the project. We will disseminate information on ethics and protocols to all interested parties.
- We are committed to sharing resources wherever possible.

Confidentiality

- Our interview protocols reflect well-considered handling procedures.
- Great care is taken to ensure confidentiality in the processing and storage of sensitive project material. Expert IT advice is sought as necessary.
- Our cardinal concern is to protect our interviewees and project participants (including their reputations, privacy and personal security) and to preserve them from exploitation.
- Staff working with at-risk groups undergo appropriate criminal and, if necessary, security checks.
- We have undertaken a risk analysis. We will regularly review this in the light of changing circumstances and will adapt procedures as necessary.
- We have referred all relevant documentation and protocols to legal advisors.

Evaluation

- We encourage feedback from all interested parties. We will regularly review our processes to enhance the quality and impact of our outputs.

Accessibility

- We aim to be fully accessible to our project participants and related groups.
- Our website complies with the WP3 accessibility standards and we will endeavour to provide information in alternative formats if requested.

Agreeing to give an interview involves a leap of faith – an investment of trust in the interviewer. Demonstrating that you have given thought to what can go wrong and that you have taken reasonable steps to safeguard against negative outcomes will go a long way towards reassuring the interviewee that you are a serious, responsible and trustworthy interviewer.

Prevention is better than cure

The first and most important way to safeguard against harming you, your interviewees and third parties is to refuse to record incriminating information in the first place. If your interviews contain – or there is reasonable evidence to suggest that they might contain – information about crimes that have not been processed by the courts of the relevant jurisdiction, no embargo can guarantee the confidentiality of that material – indeed, there have been cases involving the seizure of confidential interview accounts by law enforcement agencies. A single piece of incriminating information in a single interview could jeopardise the confidentiality of an entire collection and give way to a host of negative outcomes, from reputational damage for your interviewees, your colleagues, your sponsors (institution, organisation or group) and yourself, leading – in the worst case scenario – to civil damages, criminal liability, death threats and possible loss of life.

There is no way of knowing exactly what your interviewee is going to disclose, but you are likely to have some general ideas and you can take a number of steps to minimise the chances of acquiring unwanted and legally compromising material. The first is to include in your project literature (either on the summary sheet or as part of your interview protocols) a clear statement to the effect that you cannot accept information concerning unprocessed illegal activity. Depending on the nature of your interviews, you may wish formally to reiterate this at the beginning of the recording. Thereafter you should remain alert to the possibility of such disclosures emerging and prepare to terminate the interview if necessary. You will have a further opportunity to review the content after the interview. If you have any lingering concerns, bring it to the interviewee's attention and explore with them any potential repercussions. Then, if necessary, seek legal advice.

Respect

Treating others with respect and as we would wish to be treated ourselves is a founding principle of both religious and secular moral philosophy. As noted in the last section, we are all, to some extent, inclined to view each other in social categories and to adjust our behaviour accordingly. It can also be difficult to balance equality with a desire to show due respect for each interviewee. Again, the need for clearly established and uniformly observed guidelines is essential. This will help to ensure that each interviewee is afforded the same level of care and commitment, and it will enable you to demonstrate transparency and fair-dealing across the board.

Elderly or infirm

Showing respect and care for the elderly or infirm might involve taking the additional time necessary to allow them to compose themselves and to tell their story. Check in advance with a relative or carer the appropriate length for the interview. You should let them decide on a day and a time that suits them (mid-morning is usually a convenient and productive time). Take care not to rush, and avoid any hint of impatience (for example by finishing sentences or indicating that they are repeating a point). You need to be particularly alert to any sign of tiredness; offer a break after half an hour or so, and arrange to come back on another occasion if necessary. If they suffer from hearing difficulties be sure to speak up, and take extra care to eliminate background noise. If your interviewee's sight is impaired you might want to increase the font size for written communications. Diplomacy is critically important: people are very sensitive to being patronised, and they know when it is happening.

Young people

Interviewing young people calls for a special set of skills. Your approach should be practical and realistic. Straightforward questions, clearly stated, are always best, but they are particularly important when dealing with minors. In order to tap and channel the exuberance and energy of youth you might consider adapting your interviews to form part of an interactive programme – one that is structured, rewarding and fun.

ENCOUNTERS WITH YOUTHS

Having worked in the field of youth and community work for over twenty-five years, I have had the experience and privilege of interviewing numerous people both formally and informally. I also work as a counsellor and find that some techniques transfer well to interviewing.

For me, the most important stage is the first few minutes when you meet and begin to establish a relationship with a young person. This often dictates the quality of the interview. Many young people are not accustomed to being listened to, or to having their views taken seriously. We often have preconceptions about what is happening for young people: we read what the 'experts' say, and this can sometimes block our active listening.

It is important to try to meet the young person as an equal and to avoid a power imbalance. Formality can cause young people to perceive you as a figure of authority, like a parent or teacher, and this again can block effective communication. I have learned this the hard way from three of my greatest teachers – my teenage children. Parents often try to coerce their children into agreeing with what they deem to be reasonable and true, and thus fail to listen to the information that is being communicated to them. This has no place in the interview room. You must keep a check on your preconceptions, knowledge and experience, since these can influence and taint the quality of the information you receive. This is quite a challenge, especially if the attitudes or opinions being expressed are in your view misguided, ill-informed or immature.

Another lesson I have learned relates to language: keep it simple, and avoid unnecessary jargon. While excessive formality is to be avoided, so too are 'cool' terms that you would not normally use. You will most likely misplace them, and your interviewee will perceive this as a sign of falseness. In the past I have used what I considered to be 'in' teenage phrases, only to be told to 'get a life'. I eventually got the message. If I can be 'me' in the interview room, acting as genuinely and authentically as possible, then the young person is more likely to feel that they too can be themselves and tell their story.

It is also important to be aware that some young people use language which you might consider offensive, sometimes swearing as a matter of course. I find that it is generally best to let them speak in whatever terms they want to, because this tends to be conducive to a more relaxed and easy flowing type of interview. (However, as with the 'cool' terms, don't feel the need to use the same kind of language yourself. Your task is to listen, not to legitimise or judge.)

Some consideration should also be given to the gender of the young person. As the interview progresses it is important to check that your interviewee is comfortable with the language being used and the topics being discussed. For example, I have found that young men are sometimes uneasy about discussing their feelings or with expressing perceived indications of insecurity or weakness, and so I favour general phrases such as 'what was that like for you?' as opposed to 'how did that make you feel?' or 'were you scared?'

As with all interviews, processes and protocols must be explained before beginning. It is particularly important that you check to ensure that the young person has fully grasped what you have said, and I would also be conscious of straying too far from the agreed issues. It is vitally important to keep up to date with child protection policies. Our duty of care to the young person being interviewed must always take precedence. To take one example from my past experience, I interviewed a young girl in her mid-teens about the issue of bullying. Within a very short space of time she disclosed that she had taken an overdose in the past, and that she was again feeling suicidal. I have worked with a suicide awareness group and I was thus able to follow best practice. With the permission of the young person and her group coordinator, I was able to meet with her parents and to organise a referral for counselling. While this is well outside the scope of the role of an interviewer, the point is that these issues can arise from time to time, and it is important to have given prior consideration to them and to establish the correct procedures to follow before a situation arises.

Keep in mind the limitations of your role as an interviewer, and do not stray outside your level of competence or expertise. When working with young people err on the side of caution, keeping their interests to the fore. If the interview starts to move in a direction that you are not comfortable with, try and redirect the conversation, but if necessary you should consider terminating the interview and taking advice about anything that might need to be followed up (within the confines of confidentiality and the law).

One final piece of advice is to enter the interview without prior assumptions. While the majority of young people are heterosexual, many are not and it is important to avoid 'boxing them in' or judging them. More and more young people are also living with single parents, step-parents, same-sex parents and so forth, and so you should be conscious of your language and assumptions in relation to these issues. As interviewers we must be sensitive to the interviewee's cultural, ethnic and religious views and respect them. I was recently asked to carry out interviews with young people for a local education organisation. They explained that they had booked a venue and that refreshments would be provided. When I asked for further information I became aware that some of the interviewees were from the local Muslim community. The interviews had been scheduled for a Friday, which clashed with the young Muslims' prayer time, and no consideration had been given to their dietary requirements. After a short discussion we were able to reschedule and to broaden the menu; everything passed off without a hitch, but this was a simple case of making assumptions and thus failing to prepare.

It is not always easy to understand young people's choices. At the age of ten my daughter declared that she was turning vegetarian. She persisted in her choice, but my wife and I resolved to ignore it as a 'phase'. A year passed before it occurred to us to sit down and ask her what her reasons were. To our amazement she was able to explain both her ethical belief that killing animals was wrong, and also her conviction that our human digestive system (like that of our closest relative, the chimpanzee) is best suited to a vegetarian diet. Although it did not put us off our own Sunday roast, it did teach us that young people have their own beliefs and views, and these are sometimes better informed than our own. All we really have to do as interviewers is create a safe environment, assume nothing, ask open, non-judgemental questions, and then sit up, listen and learn.

Social, cultural and political considerations

Before approaching an ethnic or cultural group with which you are not wholly familiar, it makes sense to research their values, beliefs, norms and customs (dress, language, conduct). For example, nodding may not always denote 'I agree', and some religions prohibit touching between unrelated men and women, including handshaking. Approach a representative organisation to request guidance on issues that might offend. If you feel that you cannot abide by the required conditions (for example, by adopting terminology that is acceptable to the interviewee), then you should reconsider whether or not you are best placed to research this particular category.

When deciding how to dress for your interview, consider firstly the social and cultural background of your interviewee and the location of the encounter; some may view casual dress as a sign of disrespect, while others will be unnerved if you show up in a suit. However, the second and equally important concern is to ensure that you feel comfortable and self-confident.

When drafting topics for discussion in the interview, take particular care to ask open-ended questions and avoid terms that may smack of prejudice or preconceived ideas. Having conducted background research, remain alert to shifts in attitudes and assumptions. Keep abreast of issues and events affecting the group and new areas of sensitivity, and bear in mind that no matter how tight the group, there will be a range of opinions and attitudes. It is likely that there will also be sharply opposing views across sub- and splinter-groups. Be prepared to adapt your approach, and your demonstration of respect, to suit each individual and their personal circumstances.

Interviewing opposing groups

It is common to conduct interviews with members of contrasting or opposing social and political groups. Your protocols must be uniform and transparent (and you must be ready to produce them if necessary), but prudence sometimes dictates that you moderate your approach. Showing respect for and building rapport with your interviewees, while at the same time remaining true to your own values and protocols, can be challenging.

NO NEUTRALS HERE

Most individuals and groups have multiple co-existent identities – and these often change over time. But the tendency to view each other in categories and to temper our communication accordingly is almost universal. This process of 'telling' is not surprisingly more marked in sharply divided societies.

To take some examples from our own work, the very term 'Northern Ireland' is contested. Since the foundation of the state there has been a significant minority of nationalists opposed to its existence. The two main communities – nationalist and unionist – remain strongly divided along religious, cultural and political lines. A host of identifiers and symbols (forename, surname, place of birth, religious and cultural affiliation, schools attended, preferred sports, badges) will, in an instant, associate an individual with one or other tradition.

A single word – Derry or Londonderry – can classify. Other terms and designations will situate you on spectrum. Examples include: the Province,

Ulster, Northern Ireland, the North (capital N), the north (small n), the six counties; or terrorists, murderers, killers, paramilitaries, combatants, Volunteers. Negotiating the thicket of nuances and the subtleties of ethnic, religious, and political distinctions is often challenging. Similar issues arise in relation to accent and articulation: in some societies class origins are betrayed in mere syllables, and assumptions follow suit.

Choice of language can give rise to ethical issues. For example, one of our interviewers discovered half-way through an interview that a false assumption had been made about her identity. (This became evident as the interviewee offered a series of prejudiced observations about the 'other' community.) In such a case, should the interviewer halt the interview and cause considerable embarrassment, or proceed with the risk that the interviewee might later feel misled? We return to such interpersonal dynamics and dilemmas in Section 5.

Protecting confidences

Most interviews are non-controversial, but we have noted that in the course of any encounter it is possible to record information that could cause embarrassment or upset for interviewees and named third parties. Where an interviewee positively indicates that they want you to keep information confidential, generally you must do so. Where an interviewee does not make this clear, you will need to exercise sound judgement as to what can and should be made public. There are extreme occasions when you cannot agree to protect a confidence, and this should be made explicit. In certain circumstances public policy overrides the obligation of confidence. Examples include a disclosure by the interviewee of criminal wrong-doing that has not been adjudicated by the courts, or a declared intention to commit a crime such as child abuse. There may also be circumstances where you feel a moral obligation to disclose the confidence – for example, if the interviewee indicates an intention to commit suicide.

Until such time as an interviewee has formally released their interview and you have satisfied yourself that the material is fit for public consumption, you will need to take care to protect confidences. This is particularly true if you are interviewing in fraught communities or in a workplace, where a word out of place could upset an uneasy equilibrium. The more local your interviews the more easily this can happen, and no matter how laudable your intentions (raising awareness, increasing tolerance, building bridges and so on), you should not carelessly upset communal or family relations. If in doubt, seek local advice. A wise and seasoned observer will alert you to sensitivities that are not obvious to an outsider.

The temptation to share a colourful or telling anecdote is often compelling. It might make for a good story with which to regale families or friends; it could serve to shatter a popularly held myth or untruth; and correcting this (in public or private) could make you appear intelligent, well informed and interesting. There may also be a natural tendency when conducting interviews to disclose what previous interviewees have said. Depending on the topic and type of interview, this last issue need not present a problem. If the information was freely given and approved by the interviewee and it is not likely to harm or damage anyone, then you may of course refer to it. If the interviewee in question has not yet signed a consent form (for example, if they are waiting for receipt of a transcript) then you must take care not quote them by name (or in a manner that could identify them). This ability to protect confidences takes its place in an array of skills that includes social maturity, empathy, self-discipline, a sense of discretion and good judgement.

Informed consent

When you record an interview you create something. One of the first things to establish is who has rights in the product that you create. You can then proceed to apportion responsibility.

Although you have conceived of and created the research project, issued the invitation to interview, acquired and operated all necessary equipment and framed the questions that shape the encounter, you cannot assume to own all copyright in the entirety of the recording. If you want freedom to edit and make use of the full recording in the future, then you must have unambiguous ownership of it or a licence to do so. The simplest way to establish that is by asking an interviewee to assign any copyright he or she may have in the recording to you (or a named third party, if you are interviewing on behalf of another). As a minimum the assignment must be in writing and signed by the interviewee. It is advisable to have the agreement signed, witnessed and dated by both you and the interviewee. Be aware that, even if copyright has been assigned to you, the interviewee may still have moral rights in the interview. Moral rights cannot be assigned. The most significant moral rights in this context are the right to object to derogatory treatment of the interview, and the right to be identified as an author.

There is no definitive consent form; each project is different, and you will need to think carefully about the issues that are relevant to your research, the legislation of the relevant jurisdiction(s) and, of course, any agreement that you have reached with prospective interviewees. We set out below some indicative examples:

Project name:

Host institution(s) (if any)

Project description (if necessary enclose on a separate sheet)

Interviewee consent

1. The interviewer has described to me and I understand the details of the project as set out on the Project Description – what the research is about, who is undertaking it, why it is being undertaken and who is sponsoring it. I have indicated below how this interview is to be disseminated and used.
2. I agree to the recording of the interview.
3. The interviewer has informed me that I will receive a copy of the interview transcript and I will be given the opportunity to amend content, withdraw statements and to provide additional information if I wish.
4. I hereby accept this opportunity to contribute to this project and I assign any copyright I may have in my interview to Mr Jack Jones.

Signed ....
Date ....
Witnessed by ....

Use of interview material

Can we use material from your contribution for the purposes of x, y and z?

Yes/No

Can we post material from your contribution or your entire contribution on the internet?

Yes/No

Are you happy to be listed by name as an interviewee/contributor to (cite publication/film/exhibition/report/presentation etc.)?

Yes/No

[Continue as necessary]

Preservation in archives

We (INSTITUTION or INDIVIDUAL) wish to preserve your interview material by depositing copies at (NAME and/or LOCATION OF ARCHIVE). By signing this waiver you agree to copies of your interview material being deposited.

Signed ....
Date ....
Witnessed by ....

The terms of this agreement shall be governed by the law of X.

It is important to note that your chosen sound archive will require a further agreement, enabling them to catalogue, process, preserve and make accessible your interview material. As we discuss in Section 8, it is advisable to contact your nearest sound archive at the outset. They will explain the various options and requirements, and you can then adapt your consent form to accommodate your research needs, your interviewees' preferences, and the cause of long-term preservation and access.

Data protection

In addition to moral rights, your interviewees retain a right to privacy (whether or not any copyright in the interview has been assigned to you). Data protection legislation applies to the processing of personal information, which includes data relating to living individuals who can be identified from that data – for example, names, addresses, telephone numbers, job titles, dates of birth and so on. It can also include expressions of opinion – whether expressed by them, or concerning them.

Depending on the nature and volume of information that you plan to collect, create and store, the person or institution responsible for controlling that information may need to notify the Information Commissioner's Office or the equivalent organisation in the appropriate jurisdiction(s), listing the relevant classes of information and the purposes for which they will be processed.

The data controller is the person who (either alone, jointly or in common with others) determines the purposes for which and the manner in which any personal data is (or will be) processed. This might be a company, a university or an employer, or it may be the interviewer's sole responsibility. If you involve third parties, such as transcribers, they may be classified as data processors and they may have obligations under the terms of this legislation. This should be clearly outlined to them before undertaking the work, and they must be aware of their responsibility to safeguard the personal data that they process. In addition, they should be required by a written contract to comply with applicable data processing legislation and to apply appropriate security measures.

You should also make it clear to your interviewees (both in the project summary and on the consent form) where you plan to store information relating to them and who will have access to it. For example, if you plan to process and store the information on a computer connected to a college network, the college, as the host of that information, will have access to it and your interviewee has a right to know this.

There are a number of key principles underpinning data protection legislation in the EU. These require that:

- Data must be processed fairly and lawfully
- Data must be obtained only for specified lawful purposes and not further processed in a manner which is incompatible with those purposes

- Data must be adequate, relevant and not excessive in relation to the purposes for which it is processed
- Data must be accurate and, where necessary, kept up to date. Generally, controllers are required to update databases unless they constitute a static archive
- Data must not be kept for longer than necessary
- Data must be processed in accordance with the rights of data subjects under the relevant data protection legislation
- Appropriate technical and organisational security measures must be taken to prevent unauthorised or unlawful processing, accidental loss, destruction or damage of personal data
- When transferring personal data outside the European Economic Area, you must ensure that the destination country can offer an adequate level of protection for the rights of the data subject in relation to the processing of personal data.

Data protection law understandably imposes more onerous requirements on the processing of sensitive personal data. Sensitive personal data consists of information about the data subject's racial or ethnic origin, political opinions, religious or similar beliefs, trade union membership, physical or mental health or condition, sexual life, or commission of or proceedings for any offence committed or alleged to have been committed by the data subject. It is quite possible that your interviews will contain such information, and it is thus imperative that your consent form outlines the type of data to be collected and the purpose for which it is being preserved. It is vital that the interviewee positively indicates that they agree that you may collect, process and preserve this information (subject to the qualifications referred to in Section 2 relating to issues such as criminal offences).

Protecting your data from unlawful or unauthorised processing, accidental loss or destruction

As noted, you have a duty to protect data subjects' privacy by ensuring that information relating to them is stored securely. This demands that you consider who else might have access to the material, and if necessary (and as we discuss in Section 6) you must adopt security measures (strong passwords, encryption etc.) to ensure that the data is adequately protected. You should be particularly careful with regard to tablets and mobile devices (for example, smartphones containing names, addresses, phone numbers and text messages, as well as emails and attachments). These are particularly prone to theft, and you should exercise extra caution if you are using them to process or store information relating to your interviews.

This is a very brief outline of some of the key principles underpinning data protection legislation in the United Kingdom, and it is by no means definitive, not least because the legislation differs from one jurisdiction to the next and is subject to review and adaptation. Even though data protection law in the United Kingdom is based upon a European Union directive, there are variations in the implication of that directive across the member states. You must consult the website of the relevant data protection authorities, and if necessary you should make direct contact to seek reassurance and clarification about your specific research project. Many authorities now have user-friendly guides and good practice notes available to download from their websites.

3

RESOURCES

Interviewing demands energy of several kinds – technical, organisational, emotional and imaginative. It also requires genuine compassion, curiosity, a broad humane commitment and an abundance of common sense. We consider these skills and the ways in which they can be developed in Section 5. At this point we want to introduce the necessary practical components so that you can begin to develop your project budget and plan.

Planning your project

The primary investment in an interview project is time. It is difficult to imagine just how long the conduct and processing of a single interview can take, before secondary outputs are even considered.

It is best to start with the desirable and then work backwards towards what is realistically possible. Revisit your response to the question 'Where Do I Want to Go?' and list all of the possible outputs for your research. Divide these into short-, medium- and long-term goals. Then answer the following questions:

- What are my goals? (Capture information for a dissertation, article or book; record material for use in an exhibition; create a dedicated oral archive etc.)
- What are my obligations? (Fulfil an organisational requirement, compile a report)
- How much time can I devote to this project?
- What is my deadline?
- What resources do I have?
- What is my budget?
- Will I transcribe my interviews?

- Will I offer participants the opportunity to review and amend transcripts and/or recordings?

Working backwards from your completion date and available budget, decide roughly how many interviews you hope to record. The best way to establish how long each interview will take is to conduct one. A friend or relative might oblige – although this is not a 'true' encounter, it will give you some sense of the time that it takes to process a single interview. Decide on a suitable subject (perhaps a topic of mutual interest that you might not otherwise have a chance to examine). Make it as realistic as possible by finding a quiet room where you won't be disrupted, and set aside at least fifteen minutes to give you an opportunity to develop a questioning strategy.

Pilot

If your project will ultimately involve a significant investment of time and resources you might consider a scaled-down pilot. This will help you to test your proposal from a number of vantage points:

- Availability and willingness of interviewees
- Cost of securing all necessary equipment
- Your aptitude for conducting interviews (ability, interest, enjoyment)
- Time and costs involved in planning, conducting and processing interviews (travel, subsistence, venue hire)
- Viability of and interest in proposed outputs
- Risk-benefit analysis (seek legal and other advice based on preliminary findings and issues that arise in the course of your pilot)
- Gain feedback from interviewees so as to inform your ethical framework.

This information will greatly enhance your ability to scope and plan your research. The alternative is to muddle into a project. This can work, but it may not, and even if it does, learning as you go may entail costs in terms of both opportunity and resources.

Transcription

Interviewees will generally welcome an opportunity to reflect on what they have said. You can then draw on an agreed version of their input to support an end product. You can do this either by giving your interviewee a copy of the recording, or by supplying a transcript.

Transcription is time-consuming and (if you decide to out-source the service) can be costly. Before commencing you might want to experiment with speech recognition software programmes. Because we interview across a range of dialects and accents we have not found these programmes to be particularly useful, but they are improving all the time (and most software companies offer a free trial).

No matter how faithful the transcript, it is at best a translation of what transpired in the course of the interview. Punctuation changes meaning, as does any element of formalisation. A significant amount of communication is non-verbal, and it is simply impossible to reproduce this in the text. There are conventions for transcription, of course; for example, you can use ellipses and square brackets […] to indicate pauses, and then simply state if there is a longer break in proceedings.

The extent to which you want to produce a verbatim transcript depends on your objective. If dialect is a primary interest, and you are strongly opposed to any deviation from the actual words uttered, then you will need to establish a uniform system for the representation of slang or vernacular words and phrases. You might find it helpful to consult one of the many dictionaries of slang now on the market. It will also aid future users of the data if you keep a log of commonly-used terms and their meaning (for example, 'youns', meaning 'you ones' or 'you' plural; 'weans', meaning 'wee ones' or 'young children'). You can either insert the meaning in square brackets after the term, or provide an index that you save and deposit alongside the transcripts.

As we discuss in Section 9, grammatical errors present more of a problem. If your interviewee states, 'What I done was this…' or 'I seen a film the other week that put me in mind of them days', do you correct the grammar before sending it back for review? The inclination of most transcribers, researchers and scholars is to remain as faithful as possible to the spoken word. However, you should be aware that some interviewees will be quite taken aback – embarrassed and even shocked and insulted – to receive a script that retains obvious grammatical errors. If you plan to produce a verbatim script, it is therefore vital that you forewarn the interviewee. You might want to explain that although your interviews conform to a fairly formal design, the actual encounter in many ways resembles a conversation, with all the variations and discontinuities thereof. Tell them that interviewees are often a little dismayed when they see their informal speech transcribed on a page, and reassure them as to the value of their contribution.

What to look for in a transcriber

Apart from the necessary competencies and skills, the most important thing to look for in a transcriber is maturity and discretion. All of your attention to detail in safeguarding the confidentiality of your material and respecting the privacy of your interviewees will amount to nothing if you invite into your camp a talkative and indiscreet typist. The best way to establish credentials is by taking references from former clients and by talking through your concerns with the individual concerned. You will quickly get a sense of their understanding of the repercussions of a word out of place. You will also be able to judge the extent to which their career and livelihood depends on a reputation for confidentiality. If this is simply a 'filler', a quick means of making money on the side, they may not be overly concerned if one of your interviewees is devastated by the outing of a sensitive anecdote. If, on the other hand, they have handled confidential data in the past and come with reassurances about their mature judgement and dependability, then you are most likely in safe hands. Government employees and medical and legal secretaries will most likely be accustomed to handling confidential data.

Essential skills include speedy and accurate typing (ask for their rate per minute for audio typing) and an ear for accents. This is a skilled task, and you will ideally want to engage someone with experience of audio-transcription. (The first transcriber we employed struggled to discern the myriad personalities and organisations mentioned in the interviews. It quickly became apparent that the appointment was not cost-effective; we invested so much time in correction that it would have been quicker to do the transcription ourselves. Thereafter we sought a typist who had some familiarity with the issues and events under investigation.)

As noted, it is imperative that you ask your transcriber to sign a formal agreement setting out the terms and conditions attaching to the assignment. These should include an undertaking to maintain at all times a thoroughly discreet and responsible attitude to all matters affecting the interviews/project, to abide by any specific security protocols, and to adhere to data protection obligations.

Transcription formats

We discuss in Section 8 the importance of describing and cataloguing your files. This is particularly true of transcripts, because you may have more than one version for a single audio recording (original, verbatim, revised, agreed). It is also important regularly to check that the number on your transcript tallies with that assigned to the original recording. Once your interviews begin to stack up it is very easy to lose track of the sequence, especially if there is more than one interviewer working on the project. If you are processing a high volume of interviews it is good practice to assign one day a month to such housekeeping duties. There is no established standard for formatting transcripts, but you might want to consider something like this:

Project Logo/Title

Confidential

Mrs Olive Fisher
Interview

13 December 2013

No. 25	Olive Fisher	13 Dec 2013

Attendees:

Mrs Olive Fisher:	OF
Mr John Fitzsimons:	JF

Basic Information

Address:	3 Green Road, Ballynoggin, Dublin 8
Telephone:	+353-1-1234567 / +353 87 123456
Email:	olivefisher@yazz.ie
Date of birth:	25 June 1929

JF: *Okay, so just for the archive, I am going to state that it is the 13th of December 2013, my name is John Fitzsimons, and I'm here in St. Mary's College in Ballynoggin, Dublin, interviewing Mrs Olive Fisher. We'll be talking about her experience as a teacher here in the school and in particular her memories of the Blitz. I was hoping to ask you to begin, Olive, by telling me a little bit about your background, your own education and experience growing up.*

OF: Sure, well I was born in County Galway – on the outskirts of a small village called Castlecromack. You'd hardly recognise it now although, mind you, it's years since I've been back. The last time I visited was maybe five or six years ago – my son and his wife took me over. Most of our family emigrated but I was lucky – I got a scholarship. I was what was known as the Mistress's pet. And that was a big advantage I can tell you. If she liked you, she liked you, and if she didn't, God help you. My father was a teacher – he would have been known as 'the Master'.

JF: *What age were you then when you started teacher training? Were you in Primary School up until that?*

OF: I was. It was a different system altogether. Miss Madden, when the time came, suggested that I go in for what was known as JAM – Junior Assistant Mistress. And I was delighted to do it. What it entailed was…

TIPS FROM A PROFESSIONAL TRANSCRIBER

Having spent ten years in the transcription industry I have had literally thousands of audio interviews pass through my fingers.

When a new client calls, my first concern is the quality of their recordings. Very often it is too late and the deed is done. However, if they are simply seeking a quote and have not yet started recording, I remind them that, while most transcribers can increase the volume of recordings and remove a certain amount of distortion or hiss, there is simply no substitute for the careful preparation that results in a good quality recording. Sub-standard recordings may also incur a higher charge per audio minute since they take longer to transcribe.

I set out below some of my tips for achieving the best possible recording.

Recording

Analogue recorders are susceptible to mechanical wear and tear, cassette damage, motor noise and interruption by virtue of changing tapes. They are also becoming obsolete. If your budget allows, opt for a good quality digital voice recorder. A wide selection of these is now available on the market. If your budget is limited you might want to consider downloading a free app for your smartphone; these can produce quality recordings, and free software is also available to download for your laptop computer or tablet. You will need to research and test these options before you start. Similarly, you must familiarise yourself with the voice recorder before using it "live". <u>Always read the manual!</u>

Try to choose a location with minimal background noise – away from open windows or doors that overlook busy streets. Rooms with soft furnishings reduce echo, so a cosy office or living room is better than a hall or classroom.

<u>Always</u> test the recorder prior to each individual use, and listen back to the test recording with earphones to ensure that the quality is satisfactory. We can easily filter out unwanted background noise when we're listening to someone speak, but a voice recorder captures everything.

Carry a set of spare batteries and/or an extension lead of good length (four to five metres). Fail to prepare, prepare to fail!

Many interviewers run two recording devices for each interview. All too often I have heard horror stories about lengthy and invaluable accounts being lost due to lack of preparation and back-up.

If you are interviewing more than one person, position the recorder or microphone the same distance from each person speaking and as far away as possible from any noise-creating objects. If relying on an internal microphone, pay particular attention to the location of the microphone on the recorder unit. In a one-on-one interview, position it closer to the interviewee as their responses are more important than the questions.

Look out for factors that may create unwanted noise. Some examples include: teacups on saucers or cutlery on plates near the recorder, fingers drumming on the table, participants' feet tapping on a wooden floor, squeaking chairs, nearby air conditioning units or fans, open windows, coughing or sneezing. Placing a cushion underneath the recorder (or even a hat, scarf or glove) will help to reduce unwanted noise travelling through the surface on which it is resting.

You want your interviewee to be comfortable with the presence of the recorder, but at the same time to talk as if it wasn't there. You, on the other hand, should be very aware that it is there, and you must remain vigilant for external factors that might render parts of the recording unintelligible. For example, if your interviewee is responding to your question and a car horn sounds from outside a nearby window, it can make the response to a question useless. For example:

> I: What do you think of the rate of income tax in the country?
> R: I think the income tax rate is [BEEP!] too high.

Did the interviewee say "way too high" or "not too high"? These possible responses are conflicting.

To combat this, on hearing the interruption, and rather than asking the subject to repeat themselves, you can confirm by repetition. For example:

> I: What do you think of the rate of income tax in the country?
> R: I think the rate of tax is [BEEP!] too high.
> I: Okay, so you think the rate is not too high.

Have you ever noticed that when you whisper at someone, they tend to whisper back? For this reason, you should speak in a clear tone, not too fast and without muttering. This will encourage your interviewee to do the same.

Facilitating clear and accurate transcription

As you record your interviews, listen out for jargon or slang words. After the interview, jot down as many of them as you can remember. Supplying a 'glossary' to your transcriber will help reduce the amount of unknown or misheard words or phrases. If you plan to do a significant number of interviews on a set topic such as enlistment in the Second World War, it is also worth supplying your transcription company with some background literature. This should help to familiarise them with the subject matter and with key terms and place names.

Conventions

Most transcription companies will have their own standard 'conventions'. Ours are set out below.

TRANSCRIPTION CONVENTIONS

1. We do not change any identifying details in the initial stages of transcription; we type names and place names as heard unless otherwise requested.

2. Each line represents a line of speech, and in the case of a one-on-one interview, the interviewer will be indicated using bold typeface.

3. Phonetic details are included where relevant to the analysis (or if requested); otherwise spelling is normalised.

4. We use the following conventions:

.	end of intonation unit; falling intonation
,	end of intonation unit; fall–rise intonation
?	end of intonation unit; rising intonation
!	raised pitch throughout the intonation unit
<u>underline</u>	emphatic stress; increased amplitude; careful articulation of a segment
–	self-interruption; break in the intonation unit
-	self-interruption; break in the word, sound abruptly cut off
[pause]	measured pause of greater than 0.5 seconds
[laughter]	when a participant laughs
[over-lapping]	[+time stamp] overlapping speech
[+time stamp]	uncertain or inaudible
" "	reported speech or thought

File management and transfer

While most established transcription companies can handle any type of digital audio, we prefer MP3 because it is widely-used and provides high-quality compressed format files of a manageable size. WAV files, another common format, can be up to ten times the size of MP3, and can take an inordinately long time to upload.

That said, WAV format undoubtedly maintains superior quality audio, so it is advisable to save your files as both WAV (for long-term storage) and MP3 (for transcribing/editing).

As with any files processed through and on a computer, ALWAYS ensure that you have a back-up.

Another important matter is naming conventions. It is important to decide in advance what you are going to call the audio file that contains your precious interview, and to ensure that the completed transcript uses this same name so that you can easily identify, retrieve and match them up in the future.

A good quality MP3 recording (128kbps bit rate) should use about 1MB of memory per recorded minute. So, for example, an hour-long recording should result in an MP3 of approximately 55–65MB. To check the file size, right-click the icon, select properties and the details of the file are displayed.

Once you are happy with the format and the file size, you can send your audio files for transcription using one of the many uploading facilities available on the internet, e.g. Dropbox, sendthisfile.com, yousendit.com, Google Docs and so on.

Going it alone!

If your budget does not stretch to hiring a professional to do your transcription, here are a few tips to get you started.

It is important to allow adequate time. Transcribing one hour of audio can take between four and six hours if you are a competent typist. If not, it may take up to twelve hours to transcribe a single interview.

To get started you will need some transcription software. A standard audio player such as Windows Media Player will play your audio back, but when it comes to transcribing it, this software will slow you right down as you will have to take your hands off the keyboard to stop and start the recording. There are several really good pieces of software available on the market, but the most commonly used in the industry are Express Scribe or one of the products from Olympus, such as the AS-5002 DSS Player.

The next consideration is whether or not to use a foot pedal. This really comes down to personal preference, budget and maybe typing ability. Personally I don't use a foot pedal, but I have adapted the 'function' keys on my keyboard to stop, start and rewind the recording without having to take my fingers off the keyboard. The foot pedal works in the same way, except that obviously you control these functions with your feet.

Finally, your headphones. Consider the length of time that you are going to be sitting listening, and choose a pair of headphones based on this. It can be very uncomfortable to use an inner ear headset if you are going to be sitting typing for six hours at a time. In theory you can transcribe without any headphones and just use the speakers on your computer equipment, but this can effectively double the level of background noise!

Layout

When deciding how to lay out your transcript, you need to consider what you are going to do with the finished product. Is it simply for someone to read in the future, or will you import it into analysis software? The industry standard for a one-on-one interview is that the interviewer is typed in bold and the interviewee in regular font, as below:

> **How did that change come about, Stephen?**
> I suppose it has been coming for some time anyway, but it was just a case that I didn't have the resources in the past. We just didn't have enough staff.

Most clients request that all speakers be identified, in which case the above sample would become:

> **I: How did that change come about, Stephen?**
> **S:** I suppose it has been coming for some time anyway, but it was just a case that I didn't have the resources in the past. We just didn't have enough staff.

A 'legend' is created to identify each speaker. Obviously the 'I' and the 'S' can be anything you choose (one tip to speed up the transcription process is to use one letter, number or symbol per speaker. At the end you can use the 'Find' and 'Replace' functions in Microsoft Word to change these symbols, – for example, changing all occurrences of '$' to 'Michael Lord').

Unless otherwise stipulated, we adhere to the following basic rules:

1. Transcribe verbatim into Microsoft Word or compatible software.
2. Use Times New Roman font, size 12.
3. Transcripts are to be single-spaced.
4. When particular words are indiscernible, please insert an approximate timestamp – e.g. [29m] – into the flow of the transcript.

   N.B. this does not have to be accurate to the second. Where several sentences are inaudible, one timestamp will suffice.
5. Please include any utterances, pauses, laughs, angry voice hints, changes in mood etc. that seem relevant to meaning. Include these in square brackets and italic.
6. Unless requested, you need not transcribe frequently repeated words such as 'erm' or 'like'.

The last rule listed here can be tricky. Speech disfluencies generally disrupt the flow of the transcript, but in some instances they are crucial to meaning. It is up to you as the researcher/interviewer to decide at the outset how you want this to be handled. An experienced transcriber will gladly discuss the issue with you and help you to reach a satisfactory decision.

When things go wrong...

If you prepare well in advance and test your recording equipment and the environment in which the interviews will be recorded beforehand, it is unlikely that anything will go wrong. Even if the quality of your recording is disappointing, all may not be lost. As noted, most transcription companies can increase volume, reduce background noise and generally improve the quality of your recording. They will also bring to the task their experience of discerning a range of accents and speech impediments.

Developing...

As with most skills, your competence will improve as you progress. It will most likely seem like a painfully slow process to begin with, but you will quickly gather speed and expertise.

Any transcript will always benefit from a 'second run through', so when you have typed from start to finish, set the recording back to the start and listen through again with your transcript in front of you. You will be surprised at just how many nuances you missed first time around, how many words you misheard, and how many bits that you simply could not understand now make perfect sense.

Similarly, the first few transcripts that you produce will have many mistakes and anomalies. This quality will improve as you go. Practice makes perfect!

If you resolve to transcribe your own interviews, you will need to do a trial run before finalising your time-frame and budget. This involves typing out a set five-minute piece of audio (for example, a pre-recorded piece from the radio or television, or an interview that you listen to on the internet). You may wish to repeat the exercise to see how quickly your typing gathers speed. Record your average typing time for the set piece, scale this up to a one-hour interview and multiply by the number of interviews that you hope to record.

It is also important to decide at the outset whether or not you plan to issue a review copy. If you want to offer this, you must allow for printing, postage and the time that it will take for the interviewee to: a) read and edit the script; and b) return it. If you cannot collect the revised script in person, you must budget for the inclusion of stamped addressed envelopes (it is unreasonable to expect the interviewee to bear the cost of return postage, and it generally encourages a speedy return). Paper quickly gathers weight, and postage costs can be fairly steep. Unless you have postal scales (or finely calibrated kitchen scales and an up-to-date chart of postal costs) you will need to go to the Post Office and ask them to weigh the outgoing parcel and then tell you how much it will cost for the interviewee to send it back. (This can be awkward if you are sending it to another jurisdiction. In this case you will need to purchase the appropriate stamps at the time of the interview.)

Outputs

List the various outputs for your research and cost these in turn (for an exhibition, cost venue hire, set-up, hire of audio-visual equipment etc. For publications, consider image rights, indexing and copy-editing.)

Audio equipment

In practical terms you will need:

Essential:

- A good quality audio recorder
- Access to computer facilities/electronic storage (for processing and storing digital audio files, transcripts, supporting documentation, and back-up).

Highly desirable:

- Solid state recorder capable of recording uncompressed files
- Good quality microphone (ideally stick and lapel)
- Back-up recorder
- Access to sufficient electronic storage to process and store large digital files
- Expansion drive for back-up
- Headphones
- Camera
- Transcription software.

If your budget does not extend to a solid-state recorder capable of creating uncompressed PCM WAV files, opt for a widely available format such as MP3. (In an earlier research project we used an audio recorder that was supported by proprietary software. These files ultimately had to be converted to a more durable and widely available format since there was a risk that, should the company fold or withdraw that particular piece of software from their website, the recordings could become obsolete.)

If you are affiliated to a school, a college or a large organisation, investigate the possibility of borrowing equipment (consult the audio-visual or extra-mural department).

We always run a back-up device. This is not essential, but it has saved us from disasters both major and minor. (One memorable example involved an interview with a cabinet minister; for reasons yet unknown the main recorder malfunctioned.) Technology, no matter how robust, can let you down and second chances are hard to come by. If you have invested considerable time and energy in persuading an interviewee to participate in your project and you have travelled a distance to see them, a breakdown in recording equipment does not bear thinking about.

It is not essential that you photograph your interviewee, but it is well worth asking for their permission to do so as these portraits will add greatly to your final outputs (press releases, presentations to community members, exhibitions, print publications, archive collections etc.).

RECORDING EQUIPMENT

I work in the audio-visual department of a large organisation (with a staff of more than three thousand). When a client approaches me for advice on audio equipment the key questions are:

- What is the purpose of your interview(s)?
- How do you plan to transmit your recordings?
- What ends will your interviews serve a) in the short term and b) long term?
- What is your budget?
- What equipment do you have at your disposal or can you procure?
- Where will the interview(s) take place?
- Who will be conducting the interview(s)?
- Who is the interviewee?
- What is your level of expertise with regard to operating audio equipment?

If your interviews are designed to serve a short-term need, you may be able to rely on a relative cheap recorder or even your mobile telephone. (All major news and current affairs programmes use broadcast quality equipment, but if a reporter captures significant breaking news on a handheld device, it can still be broadcast.) However, if you want to produce decent sound and safeguard your recordings for future generations you will need to invest in proper equipment and learn to use it to best advantage.

Some years ago I was involved in setting up child abuse and rape crisis interview suites around the country. The two cardinal concerns in the design and choice of equipment were cost and simplicity. There is now available a decent range of affordable digital recorders, and the recordings can easily be uploaded to a laptop, PC, Mac or tablet via a USB port. For a solid-state (no moving parts) machine with decent professional parameters you can expect to pay a few hundred pounds.

Virtually all digital recorders use some sort of compression algorithm, and the choice of format depends on the quality required and the storage space available. Two of the most common recording formats are MP3 and WAV.

WAV is an uncompressed format, whereas MP3 is a codec that eliminates sound that humans cannot hear (by compression) whilst still giving a good approximation.

WAV files will occupy much more space on your hard drive, but they will yield a better quality of sound that is much more likely to stand the test of time. They are also less susceptible to the kind of degrading that we associate with analogue files.

Uncompressed digital audio is described by two measurements – bit depth (the digital 'word length') and sampling frequency (the audio bandwidth or frequency response as represented by the digital signal). The recommended setting for audio interviews is 16 bit/48 kHz.

Before commencing recording, consider carefully the available settings. If you use the 'automatic' setting, for example, a sudden noise (a door slamming or a lorry passing) could cause an undesirable adjustment and the loss of several key sentences.

The key to minimising unwanted external noise and maximising the acoustic quality of your recording is a decent microphone. The range is broad – from karaoke microphones costing less than ten pounds to studio microphones costing in excess of three thousand, and a wide range of possibilities in between. When selecting a model you need to consider budget, portability, ease of deployment, and the impact on your interviewee.

The microphone should ideally be procured with your audio recorder (you must at any rate ensure that the two are compatible). Many interviewers prefer the discretion of a lapel microphone, but a word of caution: take great care when attaching to ensure that the capsule is free from interference (hairs, buttons, breath). Thereafter, watch out for interviewees fidgeting with it. The alternative is a stick microphone. You will need to experiment until you ascertain the optimum distance from the speaker (the usual range is nine to twelve inches). If your main objective is to record 'perfect' sound you will need to locate and control all equipment to optimum effect. However, with interviews you need to balance audio quality against the facilitation of a successful encounter. For example, you may decide that it is better to leave a stick microphone on the table rather than having it in your interviewee's face.

An omni-directional microphone will give a better all-round pick up response, while a cardioid or directional microphone is more suited to focus recording (such as in a one-to-one interview). Dynamic microphones are less sensitive than condensers, and powered microphones tend to perform better than non-powered models. Depending on the final outputs envisaged, however, you may find that you get a perfectly good result with a relatively low-cost, non-powered model.

It is important to check your recording levels (using headphones) before you commence, just as you would prior to any live act. Have spare batteries to hand and carry a decent length of extension lead (in case the powerpoint is not close to the interviewee's preferred seat). Preparation is everything. Your ability to manage your equipment with confidence and skill is central to both the quality of your recording and the stress levels of all concerned.

Funding

A grant is both an asset and a liability. With it comes responsibility and obligation. It is important to ask yourself at the outset if you have the necessary time to meet the burden of administering and processing external funding. It is important also to be aware that you may be assuming both legal and financial responsibilities.

We have emphasised that the main resource requirement for the conduct of the interview is time. If you can support yourself whilst conducting research and you can either borrow or meet the costs of purchasing basic recording and IT equipment, you may not need a grant. Another possibility to consider is support in kind. If your research focuses on a particular organisation or group, it is worth approaching them to see if they might provide access to IT facilities and audio equipment on loan (they may be able to re-use the equipment when your project ends). In turn you can offer your time, research expertise, and a copy of your findings. They may be particularly interested in a print publication or a feature for their website, and thus be happy to meet the production costs.

If your research has a demonstrable social benefit (for example, if it will increase tolerance and understanding by raising awareness about a marginalised group in society or by building bridges between young and old), it is worth asking a practising lawyer if they would consider providing advice pro bono. Likewise, representative bodies such as victims' organisations may be willing to provide advice on ethics free of charge.

Sources of funding

The main sources of funding are public, private and gifts, and you will need to tailor your approach accordingly.

Most public funding bodies will periodically advertise calls for proposals, often under a particular theme. When looking for funding you need to keep a close eye on the relevant funders' websites. It is also advisable to sign up for email alerts, newsletters and RSS (Really Simple Syndication) feeds which will alert you to new calls, priority themes and application deadlines. You might be able to adapt some aspect of your research to suit a particular call without straying too far from your original ambitions.

Having identified a suitable funder and an appropriate call for your research proposal you must closely read the terms and conditions. Although your project may be entirely relevant to the theme of the funding call, you or your organisation may not be eligible to apply. (In some instances you must be attached to a third-level institution; in other instances your research must have an immediate and demonstrable impact.) If having read the terms and conditions and the 'Frequently Asked Questions' you are still unsure you should contact the funder. Completing applications can be very time-consuming and you thus want to be sure that you are directing your efforts at the right organisation.

You should also bear in mind that funders often complain about a shortage of good applications. By this they mean eligible, relevant, new, interesting and viable proposals that have some general character. Having determined that you are eligible to apply, you should establish a timeline for completion of the application. This involves working backwards from the deadline and allowing plenty of time to assemble the supporting documentation. If this involves contacting third parties (for example, grant officers at your host institution), plan to do this several weeks ahead of the closing date to allow time for unforeseen delays. You should also allow time at the end closely to review and amend the completed application.

Having established a realistic timeline for the application process you can concentrate on the core item: your proposal. The first thing to consider is relevance. Again, this involves studying the funding call very closely and asking how and in what ways your project is relevant to the priority theme and how it can meet the stated aims and objectives. In some cases it is possible to get clarification from the funder (there is often a designated grant officer listed on the call for applications). It is always best to seek such confirmation of relevance in writing so as to avoid disappointment or frustration down the line.

A good proposal is key. It must clearly establish the concept behind your project – its significance, usefulness and originality. It must also demonstrate that you have the means necessary to complete it. This can be done by reference to research experience or a track record of completing projects, or simply by presenting a carefully budgeted and time-bound plan of work. (Some funders will ask you to test each of your objectives in turn and to demonstrate that they are SMART (Strategic, Measurable, Achievable, Realistic, and Time-bound).

The proposal is normally the sole measure of your competence and ability, and it is thus essential that you take great care in putting it together. Aim to complete it well ahead of the application deadline, and then review it carefully for spelling, grammar and general coherence. With a flood of applications the assessors' first cut is usually based on 'who can we reject?' Any hint of a rushed or sloppy presentation will seriously erode your chances of success. If possible, ask an experienced friend or colleague to review the application. Before submitting, check that you have assembled all necessary paperwork – including, for example, the necessary signatures and stamps of approval from your host institution.

If your application is unsuccessful, do not become disheartened. It is only by applying for grants that you become familiar with the process. It is always worth asking for feedback as this may provide you with some constructive advice as to how to adapt your proposal going forward. Having taken the time carefully to plan and budget your project, you will be able to tailor your application to suit another funding call – or identify one that better suits your needs and ambitions.

Some funders are emphatic that you cannot hold an award from them in conjunction with another. In other cases it is perfectly in order to combine, for example, private and public funding together with support in kind. This is particularly common with private funding where one agency agrees to match the funding of another. In these instances a funder will want to be able to identify with a discrete element of your work.

Establishing a record

As noted, with a grant comes responsibility. Having secured your first award it is important that you establish a reputation for delivering – on budget and on time. If you fail to meet completion obligations or to administer funding in accordance with the set rules and regulations (including, for example, compliance with procurement guidelines, submission of periodic reviews, budget updates and final reports) your grant may become more of a liability than an asset. For this reason it is advisable to start with a small grant and then gradually advance to larger, more complex and closely regulated awards.

4

GROUNDWORK

Interviewing is akin to painting a wall. If you do not adequately prepare the result will be disappointing, and before too long cracks will appear. The necessary level of background research depends on the nature of the topic, the expectation of your interviewee, and the availability of information. If your subject has a public profile it should be quite easy to put together a biographical note. At the very least you should conduct some desktop research to establish a rough chronology of their career and their stance on key issues. If you have access to a printer you might want to put together a folder of relevant articles (assuming they are broadly factual and unlikely to startle or offend). This is another way of demonstrating respect for your interviewee, and of showing that you are in earnest about your project.

Nowadays most researchers commence by typing their subject's name into a search engine. For public figures this should generate leads to relevant sources – biographical cameos posted by their employer, publisher or a public body, details of books or articles that they have written or contributed to (and perhaps a direct link to the publication), links to newspaper articles containing reference to them, audio links to interviews they have given, details of their membership of organisations and boards, information about their support for particular charities or causes. The quality of source material available online is improving all the time, but you must be able to distinguish between reliable and untrustworthy sources. Continue cross-checking until you are satisfied that your information is accurate. Having conducted some preliminary research, it is worth typing your subject's name into the search engine of an online newspaper archive (most public libraries subscribe to a range of online databanks). Once you establish some key dates you can begin to work sideways, cross-checking with other primary and secondary sources. Your local library should have copies of dictionaries of national biography, Who's Who, and other relevant databases. If your subject had a well-known parent or relative it is worth pulling up their obituary and reports from the time of their death.

It is important to keep this background research in proportion. If your interviewee turns out to be peripheral (whether because the parameters of your research change or because their story is less central than at first you thought) you may subsequently feel that this time might have been better spent pressing on with other interviews. And, if the individual has not been in the public eye you may be restricted to whatever information is offered by the person or organisation that recommended them in the first place, or by the interviewee themselves (in the course of preliminary conversation).

Alongside biographical research you will need to conduct some general research on the topic under investigation and set out a timeline of key events. If the project is academic in nature you will need to engage in a comprehensive literature review and then establish a set of research questions. As you gather interviews your knowledge will grow, and it will become easier and easier to craft appropriate questions based on preliminary biographical research.

In some instances an interviewee may refuse an interview if you cannot demonstrate that you have taken the time and trouble to conduct at least some background research. This is particularly true of public figures who have committed much to the public record. They may become irritated and unresponsive if you fail to note their stance on the issues or topics under investigation; they are not there to save you a trip to the library or cut your online research time. Some might test your level of preparation in the opening five to ten minutes by asking such questions as 'Do you know much about the organisation?', 'I take it you are familiar with this particular controversy?', 'Remind me roughly what date the group was founded?' or 'Who was in government at that time, my memory fails me.'

In general, the more knowledgeable you are about both your research subject and your interviewees, the more command you will have over the interview. Background knowledge is never wasted and it need not compromise your ability to keep an open mind and let the interviewee challenge and correct the record.

If you do not have access to the resources necessary to conduct preliminary research, or if your time schedule does not allow for it, do not despair. In some situations – though they are not all that many – the 'innocent abroad' may fare better than a seasoned observer. A shy or reluctant interviewee may even be intimidated by a display of prior knowledge about the research subject, and in these situations it is especially important to wear your knowledge lightly.

Identifying and selecting interviewees

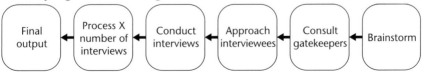

Working backwards from your ideal outputs, your budget and your timeline, establish approximately how many people you want to interview. Deciding who to select and how to approach them is the next challenge. It is often helpful to begin with a brainstorming session based on your background research and informal meetings with friends and colleagues. This will help you to establish a preliminary 'wish-list'.

Your target list of interviewees may be self-evident (for example, past pupils of a particular school, former employees of a given factory, those who were engaged in or witnessed a specific historic event) or it may be more loosely defined (focusing on a theme such as unemployment, emigration or perceptions of discrimination).

In defining your project you must ensure that your goals are attainable. For example, if you plan to conduct a nationwide study of a complex organisation you may need to restrict your attention to particular sub-categories. Likewise, if you are interested in a broad theme such as a social class phenomenon it might be advisable to restrict the geographic catchment area. You need to avoid duplication, but within your focus you must be as comprehensive as possible. This can be a tricky judgement.

Sampling

As we discuss in Section 9, the extent to which you are concerned with representation depends ultimately on the nature of your project. It depends also on your understanding of the purpose of history. Put simply, some researchers will mine their interviews for hard, verifiable and comparable data, while others will be more interested in form and meaning – on how and why information is presented. More still will show awareness and interest in both.

In the opening section we emphasised the range of disciplines and activities and purposes for which interviews are employed. If your aim is to conduct a narrative analysis of life-story interviews – to study the language, form, genre and meaning therein – it will make sense to let your interviewee dictate their story without interruption. You may be more interested in individual insights than the extent to which their experience is typical. If, on the other hand, you want to conduct comprehensive research on a topic or theme and to compare the responses of a variety of interviewees, you will need to introduce some structure.

Sampling procedures can be random, stratified or systematic (a good example of the latter is Paul Thompson's use of the 1911 census to select 444 informants for his study of family and life in Edwardian Britain).

The matrix

Our interviews have, for the most part, been semi-structured (both in terms of design and content). We identified at the outset a list of potential categories and sub-categories. An indicative model is set out opposite.

STUDY OF THE FASHION INDUSTRY
Matrix of potential interviewees
▨ Interview complete   ▪ Agreed to interview   ■ Refused interview

DESIGN				
Fashion designers	Fashion forecasters	Textile designers	Design directors	Fashion illustrators

PRODUCTION					
Textiles manufacturers	Yarn manufacturers	Production managers	Factory owners	Tailors	Product sourcing

PURCHASING									
Sales staff	Sales reps	Financial merchandisers			Buyers				
		Analytical purchasing	Quantitative analysis of purchasing	Purchasing forecasting	High street	Dept. stores	Boutiques	Online	

MERCHANDISING								
Store manager	PR & Marketing				Display			
	Publicists	Event planners	Media reps	Market researchers	Creative director	Creative team members	Window, prop and mannequin stytlists	

MEDIA								
Media planners	Campaign managers	Publicists	Social media managers	Print			Radio/ television	
				Magazine editors	Bloggers	Fashion columnists		

FASHION MARKET					
Economists	Department store owners	Boutique owners	Retail barometers	Financial merchandisers	Forecasters

MANAGEMENT				
Stores	Boutiques	Buying controllers	Showroom managers	HR

GENERAL PUBLIC									
Female					Male				
12–17	18–24	25–39	40–59	60+	12–17	18–24	25–39	40–59	60+

This grid is merely notional. You will obviously need to develop categories and sub-categories to suit your own research. Once you have established these you can introduce geographic boundaries, time periods and so forth. You might then apportion a target number of interviewees for each category. If you are more interested in coverage than numerical representation, you may wish to give weighted priority to obscure and understudied fields.

This enables you to establish a focused 'wish-list' of interviewees. The next step is a slightly macabre one. Common sense dictates that you prioritise the elderly and frail. (Depending on the sense of urgency, you may even wish to conduct one or two interviews with elderly witnesses ahead of the launch of the project proper.)

Common sense also dictates that you start with the low-hanging fruit: those that are ready and willing to commit an interview. A well-disposed, informative and self-confident individual can all but interview themselves. You need simply to show up, turn on the recorder, and kick-start a fascinating discussion. Once you have a few such interviews under your belt your confidence in operating the equipment, handling the paperwork and executing an interview will grow – and so too will your track record. One successful interview opens the door to the next.

Approaching interviewees

As noted above, the manner in which you approach your interviewees will depend on the degree to which you are concerned with representation. Here we set out some commonly employed strategies.

In many instances it is possible and appropriate to approach interviewees directly (through a relative, neighbour, colleague or other contact). Although the first step may be a casual face-to-face encounter, it is important to offer a formal written summary of your aims and objectives, the interview protocols, and the full range of anticipated outcomes. This helps to avoid confusion, disappointment or missed expectations down the line (bearing in mind that the potential for upset may be all the greater if your interviewee is known to you or has been recommended by a friend). It is much better that an interviewee takes some time to consider the invitation and to ask for clarification and reassurance before committing you both to a considerable investment of time, energy and resources.

Another possibility is to post an advertisement in a local or national newspaper, parish newsletter, website, local library, organisation's magazine, or on the noticeboard of a local supermarket, post office or day-centre. Alternatively, you might get permission to send a group email to the staff or membership of relevant organisations. It is advisable to state in your communication that you may not be able to interview all who volunteer. It is also important to be transparent about your rationale for selection. (The husband of one of our interviewees was confounded as to why he had not been selected for interview. The project in hand focused on female factory workers, and unfortunately time and resources did not allow his story to be captured.)

For most projects you will need to approach interviewees by way of an agency or a third party. We often refer to these as 'gatekeepers'. In some cases the gatekeeper is a representative body such as a trades union or victims' rights group. In the course of setting up complex inter-jurisdictional projects that span numerous categories and time periods, we have engaged in endless meetings with gatekeeper organisations. Building and retaining trust with these groups and individuals was an essential pre-requisite to accessing the desired range of witnesses. These organisations exist to protect members' interests, and they are understandably concerned to ensure that your research is bona fide, you have no ulterior motive, you are trustworthy and honest, you have carefully considered all possible risks for your interviewees, and you have established appropriate safeguards. Such meetings are also invaluable by way of background research; it is important to remember that gatekeepers are there to assist as well as to filter. They will alert you to existing research that may inform or alter the course of your project, and they will most likely highlight key issues, events and individuals.

A word of caution, however: if you want to access a diverse range of interviewees, leave the gatekeeper at the gates. Otherwise you will end up recording only those individuals connected to and favoured by your host. If you want to focus on that particular sub-group this need not be a problem (as a relative insider you may well be able to access a level of detail that others cannot), but if you want to include other voices you will need to maintain a degree of independence.

The snowball: advantages and disadvantages

Once you have gained access to your first round of interviewees you should find that one interviewee leads to another. (Remember to ask at the end if there is anyone else that the interviewee can recommend.) This is heartening and encouraging, but it can also present a hazard. It is important periodically to stop and review your stock of interviewees. Review the categories and weightings established at the outset, and check that you are targeting roughly the right proportion from each group. Remember that your 'matrix' of interviewees is a crude instrument; it really just contains nodules of information, and it must be subject to regular refinement in the light of the information that you gather, new possibilities, and fresh perspectives.

If you find that you are getting a lot of repetition, consider the need for access to unheard or long since forgotten voices and amend your plan accordingly. One of the core strengths of this methodology is that you have the ability to target and shape your research as you go, and thus to seek out new and fresh angles. Your original plan may well need to be adapted if those that you want to interview are either unavailable or unwilling, if you discover that similar research has already been conducted, or if new and better lines of enquiry come into view. The final tally of interviewees will represent a targeted trade-off between the desirable and the possible.

Advisory committee

For large-scale projects an advisory committee can be invaluable. They can provide a sounding board, the benefit of experience, suggest categories, themes and potential interviewees, open doors, legitimise, and help to ensure that your methods and processes are transparent. They need not assume executive authority (or responsibility) for your decisions and actions, and neither does the time commitment need to be onerous (even an annual meeting is worth having). A fresh pair of eyes and a measure of detachment will help you to stand back from your data and shape the project to best advantage.

Project summary

Your written project description should set out clearly the following information:

- Your name
- Your position (independent researcher, project director, pupil, family researcher, documentary maker, postgraduate student, journalist etc.)
- Your affiliation (organisation, group, school, third level institution)
- Your background (any previous experience of conducting research or other relevant information)

- Your sponsor (set out how the work is being financed and by whom. If appropriate, refer to individuals or institutions who have agreed to vouch for your credentials. You may wish to include a separate 'reference' from a sponsor).

The last point is important. No matter how inconvenient it might seem, you must at all times be honest and forthright – otherwise people will think that you are cheating them. This is particularly important if you are interviewing across a range of opposing groups. Some may be reassured by your sponsors; others may view them (and by extension you) with suspicion.

You need then to include a short summary of the scale, scope and nature of the topic – what you want to investigate and why. This should include a rough estimation of the number of people you hope to interview, the timeframe for completion, and all projected outcomes (exhibition, publication, archive collection etc.). If you plan to apply a particular type of analysis it is best to state this, offering illustrations if necessary.

Interview protocol

You should now set out clearly how you plan to conduct the interviews – where they will take place, how you will record them, how you will store them, what type of consent form you will ask the interviewee to sign, whether or not they will have the right to review and edit their accounts, whether the original recording and/or transcript will be preserved, who will have access to these documents (in the short- and long-term), whether or not you wish to take a photograph of your interviewee, how exactly the interview material will be edited and used, and for what purpose.

Approach letters

Get your initial approach absolutely right – often there are no second chances. You can draw up a standard letter, but you must then tailor it for each individual, striking the appropriate balance between friendliness and formality. Pay particular attention to grammar and the spelling of names, titles, decorations and awards. (Consult reliable sources: do not rely solely on internet search-engines). If you do not take the time to check and correct these simple details it will be difficult to persuade an interviewee that you are a serious, responsible and mature individual with a special interest in their experience. Be very careful to ensure that your letter is precisely and only addressed to your intended interviewee – a leftover phrase, date or name from an earlier letter will make you look careless and incompetent.

A typical approach letter will address the following issues:

Why me?

Explain why you are approaching this individual (for example, the particular relevance of their experience, a recommendation from a colleague or another participant in the research).

Why you?

It will not help your cause to list every conceivable risk in a letter of invitation, but it worth enclosing a brief summary your interview protocols and any assurances that you can offer. This might include reference to your previous experience, those individuals who can vouch for your good name and word, and the manner in which you plan to protect and safeguard the material that you collect.

What are the benefits?

Convince the individual that this project is worthwhile, and justify their commitment of time and energy. Explain the significance and purpose of the proposed interview (informing a historical analysis, preserving their unique experiences and perspective, informing a policy debate, helping to shape a report). If you plan to deposit your interviews in an archive it is worth reminding interviewees of the considerable impact that their voice will have on those who listen to the recordings in decades to come. If you feel that the group, category or class that this individual represents has been overlooked, you might want to present this an opportunity to close that gap. Beyond this, you must remember that unless you have a budget to pay interviewees you are essentially asking them for a favour. Explain how much you would appreciate an interview, and offer to answer any further questions or queries that they may have.

How much time will it take?

Include a rough timeframe – when you hope to record the interview, how long it is likely to last, when they can hope to receive a transcript, and when you plan to exhibit the outputs.

Schedules of topics

We generally craft an outline of topics for each individual interviewee. This is a time-consuming process involving considerable research, reflection and redrafting. As noted above, we begin with biographical research on both the individual concerned and the organisation or interest group that they represent. If possible we set out a timeline of key dates and issues. We then attempt to marry a life-history approach with a focus on the particular topics of interest. We begin with introductory questions designed to draw out the individual's background and to elaborate their biographical notes (we ask for corrections, further information or clarifications). We then set out the topics that we feel the interviewee is best placed to speak about. As discussed in Section 5, it is generally best to ask clear, concise and open-ended questions with follow ups as necessary. Depending on the age and experience of the interviewee and the focus of your research, you may wish to divide your questions into sections such as 'Early Life', 'Education', 'Early Days as a Teacher', 'Trip to Africa', 'McAfee Controversy', 'Parenthood', 'Back to Durham', 'Retirement' and 'General Questions'.

Our closing questions are really reminders to ourselves, and they tend to include the following:

- Are there topics of importance that we have not raised with you?
- Do you have any recommendations as to persons we might contact?
- Is there any published material to which we should pay particular attention?
- Do you have any relevant documentation (notes, memoirs, copies of material, press cuttings, etc.) which we might see and copy?
- Are you willing to let us take your photograph to deposit with your interview?
- Will you please sign our consent form?

Interviews can stir up memories of precious documentary material in the interviewee's possession. It is always worth asking if an interviewee has documentation that they might let you copy. In doing so you must take care not to exploit the interviewee in any way; if the material they hold is sensitive and you feel that bringing it to public view might distress them in any way, you should not push this issue. In many instances, though, they are only too delighted to share documents and memorabilia and you can thus be of some service both to them and to history. Nowadays it is relatively cheap to scan and copy documents, and unless they want to deposit the material in an archive your interviewee can hold on to the originals. (One of our interviewees mentioned that he held a collection of secret and coded prison diaries. These were subsequently edited and published with his cooperation.)

While the crafting of a schedule of topics is generally helpful, there are pros and cons to issuing it ahead of the encounter. If the interviewee is worried about being 'caught off-guard' or forced to disclose something that they will later regret, it can offer considerable reassurance. Some interviewees (mainly politicians) request a list of topics as a precondition to granting an interview. Remember that the schedule is at least a line on your calling-card – it shows your level of preparation and commitment to the interview.

We rarely follow these outlines to the letter, and always make it clear at point of issue that it is intended simply as an aide-memoire rather than a questionnaire. A live interview inevitably takes on a life of its own, and it is only at the end that we glance back at the list to check if there are important topics that have not been covered in the course of the discussion. That said, there have certainly been some occasions on which the interviewee treated the schedule like a questionnaire, scribbling answers on the sheets. As we discuss in Section 9, there is a danger of pre-empting or colouring memories by imposing a pre-ordained structure. We are thus increasingly inclined to simply list the topics of interest as part of our own interview preparation, and then bring along the list as an aide on the day.

Example of a formal schedule of topics:

Archbishop George Jones

6 July 2014

The Most Revd Dr George St John Jones, Archbishop of New Zealand, was born in Auckland City on 24 October 1952. He was educated at Parkhurst Royal School, Brisbane (1963–1971); Trinity College, Cambridge (1972–1975: First Class Hons in Classics, Moderatorship with Gold Medal); St. John's College, Cambridge (1981–1984: First Class Hons in Theological and Religious Studies); 1987: PhD awarded for a thesis on 'Transformation in the Age of Saint Augustine'; The Church of New Zealand Theological College, Auckland (1990). Married to Jo Hurst, a solicitor who was born in Sussex; they have two sons, Richard and Basil.

Key Dates

1983	Ordained as Deacon to the Anglican ministry
1984	Ordained as a Priest
1988	Curate at Zion Parish, Auckland, and Chaplain at Auckland City Hospital
1997–2000	Chair of the National Committee for Social Theology
24 April 2004	Elected Bishop of Auckland
	Member of the New Zealand Council of Religious Leaders
2004	Chairman of the Anglican Gospel Project
2007	Keynote speech at International Conference 'Living the Gospel in the Twenty-First Century'

Background

Your experience of communities, culture, identities growing up in New Zealand.

Role of the education system in accentuating class, cultural and religious divisions.

Historically, theological issues were a force in division and conflict. To what extent is this still the case?

Religion as a banner for other types of divisions, fears and animosities. Transcendent identities, interests.

What types of assistance were you able to provide for your flock (pastoral, material, other)?

Was your involvement in inter-faith dialogue a case of design or necessity? Where was there cause for optimism/pessimism?

Attitude of various Protestant denominations to inter-faith dialogue.

As a minority denomination in New Zealand, do Anglicans have a distinctive contribution to make to peace and reconciliation? Can you offer examples?

What were the principal sins of segregation (stereotyping/dehumanisation/fear/ ignorance etc.)?
Do you feel that the Churches did enough to emphasise moral agency and individual responsibility?

In what way do Church leaders differ from politicians in their approach to negotiations?

In what ways did your work in England as a student and as a chaplain broaden your perspectives?

Can you tell us a little bit about the background to your appointment as Chair of the Anglican Gospel Project?

How did you reconcile your various responsibilities – to the Church, to your flock, to your family, to society? Could you provide examples in your answers?

To what extent has Christianity failed in its New Zealand mission? What have been its successes?

What is and might be the effect of unbelief and secularism?

General

Are there topics of importance that we have not raised with you?

Are there documents/publications to which we should pay particular attention?
Do you have any relevant documentation (notes, memoirs, copies of material, press cuttings, etc.) which we might see and copy?

Do you have any particular recommendations as to persons we might contact?

Would you be willing to let us take your photograph to deposit with your interview?

Will you please sign our consent form?

The schedule of topics set out above is quite formal. It is tuned and tailored to suit the (fictitious) Archbishop. It includes questions about theology that would be inappropriate and quite possibly intimidating for other interviewees. However, it is our experience that in order to get the best from an interviewee you need to enter into their world, and to ask questions that speak to their particular expertise. In a relatively short space of time (one to two hours) you want to encourage the interviewee to reflect deeply and meaningfully on their experiences. It would be in many ways pointless to ask a theologian a series of bland political questions. He or she would be as well placed as anyone to respond to them, but it is generally best to invite them to address the issues that are most central to their lives. For example, you will demonstrate respect and genuine interest by asking a Methodist minister questions that show some awareness or appreciation of the particular tenets of the Methodist tradition – and you will thus encourage him to give you a worthwhile interview. If you are part of a team it makes sense to play to your relative strengths and to allocate interviews accordingly.

Example of a short schedule

Background

Education, employment, trades union membership and community work

To what extent were sectarian allegiances kept outside the factory gates?

What were the main challenges?

To what extent are those born in Northern Ireland hardwired for sectarianism?

Is it possible for class issues to transcend the religious/political divide?

What is your brightest memory as a trades unionist?

The corrollary – your bleakest memory?

Shipstreet Lock-Out: recollections and reflections.

General

Are there topics of importance that we have not raised with you?

Are there documents/publications to which we should pay particular attention?

Do you have any relevant documentation (notes, memoirs, copies of material, press cuttings, etc.) which we might see and copy?

Do you have any particular recommendations as to persons we might contact?

Would you be willing to let us take your photograph to deposit with your interview?

Will you please sign our waiver?

Bubble schedules

It can also be helpful to set out your topics in linked bubbles. This enables you to see the main points at a glance and to raise related issues as and when required.

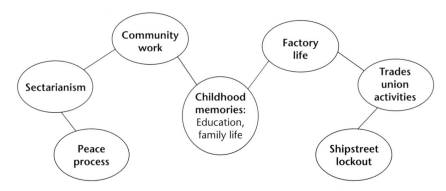

On the day

Having issued an approach letter together with a project summary and information about your protocols and procedures (including any reassurances that you wish to offer), you will, if all goes well, receive confirmation that the interviewee is willing to see you. Where possible, allow the interviewee to choose the venue. Some people are most comfortable in their own homes, but others value their privacy above all else. If the distance is manageable you could offer a quiet room at your workplace, but if you are travelling to see the interviewee, you will need to identify a suitable venue and arrange to hire a room if necessary.

Think carefully before offering a venue. Ensure that it is neutral, quiet, comfortable and therefore conducive to a discreet and relaxing exchange. You want as few distractions as possible, so avoid locations that are likely to be disruptive; you need to have some control over the space if it is somewhere other than the interviewee's home. (If possible put a 'Do not disturb' /'Interview in progress' sign on the door.) Give as much latitude as possible with dates and timings – the interviewee is doing you a favour, and you must be as accommodating as possible.

Having fixed an appropriate date, time and venue, be sure to ask for clear directions and an estimation of how long it might take to get there. It is also vitally important that you get a direct contact phone number so that you can contact your interviewee if you run into unforeseen difficulties. Likewise, make sure that your interviewee has a contact number for you in case they need to cancel at the last minute.

Before setting out plan your route carefully, leaving plenty of time for potential mishaps (missing a connecting bus, puncture, traffic jam etc.). You should aim to arrive in the immediate vicinity at least half an hour before the interview to give yourself time to compose yourself and to check that all of your equipment is in order. Interviews can be exhausting, and it is thus important that you are well rested beforehand. (If you are unwell, cancel. This is particularly important if your interviewee is elderly, or if they have small children.) An interviewee can bring things to a halt if they start to feel tired, but you must remain bright-eyed and vigilant throughout. Depending on the nature of the research, the extent to which the interviewee is inconvenienced and your available budget, you may want to consider bringing a gift (such as a small box of chocolates or biscuits).

Before setting out:

- Ensure that someone knows where you are going, who you are going to see, how you can be contacted, and what time you are likely to return (see Safety Guidelines)
- Check for any potential disruption to your travel plan, /ensure that you have sufficient fuel etc.

- If appropriate, call ahead to confirm the appointment
- Review your list of topics and any background research
- Check that all equipment is in good working order (always run a check)

Pack:

- Audio recorder
  - ○ Memory card and spares (if not built-in)
  - ○ AC adapter/cables
  - ○ Spare batteries
  - ○ Extension lead
  - ○ Back-up recorder (if available); spare memory cards and batteries
- Microphone (cable, stand, spare batteries, as necessary)
- Headphones
- Folder
  - ○ ID
  - ○ Address and telephone number of interviewee
  - ○ Consent form
  - ○ Interview topics
  - ○ Aides memoire (e.g. biographical notes, photographs, press cuttings)
  - ○ Copy of project summary
  - ○ Copy of interview protocols
  - ○ Endorsement (reference from sponsoring institution, employer or evidence of your earlier work)
  - ○ Notebook and pencil
- Gift (if appropriate)
- Mobile telephone
- Spare cash.

The first time I was invited to give an interview for a research project was way back in October 2004. I can still remember reading the letter. I was partly bemused and partly curious to know why somebody would want to interview me. I definitely wondered about the motivation of the interviewer and the purpose of the interview.

My main concern was the effect that my thoughts and views might have on the people I mentioned – former comrades and friends. I was also worried that my views could be taken out of context – and again I wondered how this could affect my relationship with those that I would mention.

The interviewer rang and talked through these worries with me. She also offered to send me an outline of the questions, and I found this very helpful. It's not easy out of the blue to revisit the events of fifty years ago and I wanted to prepare myself for it. I can't remember how well we stuck to the questions, but it gave me an idea of the interviewer's interests and reassured me that there wouldn't be any nasty surprises on the day.

Perhaps the main reason I agreed to do the interview was my desire to put on record some of my memories and experiences and my involvement in past events. I felt that the prohibition (under the Offences Against the State Act) of publications that could be deemed seditious or incriminating meant that the history of Ireland in the 1950s had not been accurately or adequately captured.

The interview itself was a positive experience. The interviewer put me at ease and conducted the interview like an informal chat rather than a formal question and answer session. This made the whole process easy and enjoyable, and I have to say I was hardly aware of the recording device on the table. The fact that the interview took place in my own home was a plus. It helped me to feel in control of the situation – this was very important as I wasn't sure how I would react to the stirring up of old memories. It was also very important to me to communicate accurately material that I felt was sensitive. I was grateful that the interviewer didn't rush me as I unpicked my recollections of these events and tried to explain them by putting them in the appropriate context.

One negative was the revival of painful memories. I got married shortly after coming out of prison and we had eleven children in fairly rapid succession. I worked a lot of overtime, and so for many years prison memories were locked away: I literally didn't have time to think about them. Now in my late eighties I was being invited to revisit those years. It wasn't too difficult to do this in the course of the interview, but I did find that in the weeks that followed I began waking at night. More and more memories came back: good, bad, and conflicting. Some were crystal clear and others were hazy. Then one day I picked up a blank copy book that belonged to one of my grandchildren and started to write down my recollections of these times – not in any particular order or sequence, but just as they came to me. I found this very therapeutic – it helped me to release them and the waking at night began to ease off.

I didn't discuss these aftereffects with the interviewer, but I was glad to receive a copy of the transcript. This enabled me to reflect on what I had said and to add further detail as it came back to me.

To the surprise of both of us that initial interview became the springboard for a much more detailed exploration of my time in prison. This arose due to the resurrection of my old prison diaries – again long since forgotten. This was interesting because together we were then able to delve deeper into that time and to question some of my initial recollections based on the documents that I had kept at the time. I have to say that my family was quite happy for me to get these things off my chest and thus to offload some 'baggage'. I really enjoyed the interviews in the end. It was definitely a worthwhile experience.

5

DEVELOPING TECHNIQUE

In the opening section we emphasised that you are already an experienced interviewer and that you need simply to build on attributes you already have. But you cannot assume talent. Some individuals have a natural abundance of common sense and social intelligence (often distinct from academic ability). Others need to hone these skills.

Developing technique involves consideration and practice. The key is active listening. This goes well beyond hearing; it is a highly developed skill demanding full concentration. You must listen not just to the words, but also to tone, implied references, and what is not said. Folded arms, monosyllabic answers, avoiding eye-contact, nervous twitching – all of these communicate a great deal, and you should respond accordingly.

On arrival

The first few minutes of an interview are generally the most challenging. You must introduce yourself, make a good impression, and encourage your interviewee to relax. It is important to take your cue from them. Some people are naturally affectionate and inclined to greet with a warm embrace. Others would melt with embarrassment (or take offence) if you were to hug or kiss them on arrival. Avoid using first names until your interviewee indicates that it is in order to do so (many people will be mildly offended if you fail to adopt their title – be it Mr, Mrs, Ms, Miss, Dr, Professor, Sir, Lady, Your Grace etc.). Pay particular attention to religious and cultural sensitivities and adapt your approach accordingly.

Unless they are well known to you, familiar with the research project, and/or extremely pressed for time, the interviewee will welcome an opportunity to chat informally about you, the interview and the nature of the research. If you have not issued a schedule of topics in advance you might want to recap on some of the issues that you would like to cover.

If your interviewee is apprehensive or in any way hostile you will need to spend time reassuring them and breaking down barriers. Scan the room for clues as to their interests. Don't give in easily. At an appropriate pace and pitch, engage in light conversation (the weather, hobbies, neighbourhood, holidays, family) until you have established some kind of rapport. Humanise your research by talking about how and why you got interested in it. Listen closely for clues as to what kind of an approach is likely to work best. Do they respond well to humour? Are they quite formal and disdainful of any hint of flippancy? Are they shy? What lingering fears or apprehensions might they have? What impression are they forming of you? Can you find some common ground?

Once you feel that the interviewee has relaxed, at least to some extent, ask if they have any further questions. Take whatever time you need to set up, ensuring that your interviewee is seated comfortably and that the equipment (recorder and microphone) is working (use your headphones to check). Use your extension lead if necessary, and have spare batteries to hand. Note any potential hazards or obstacles such as an open window, a washing machine, a television or radio, and if necessary request that these be turned off. If necessary, ask if you can shift furniture (promising to put it back). This can take more nerve than one imagines, but people rarely refuse. Press 'record' and start with an easy, open-ended question.

With experience you will develop an acute sense of when there is more to tell, when it is appropriate to pause and let the interviewee delve deeper, and when to move on. You will learn to frame questions that elicit frank and meaningful responses. With growing self-confidence, you will enable your interviewees to relax and enjoy the exchange.

Truly to listen to another human being can be a liberation and a joy: it can also be draining. There is a monumental difference between asking questions (as set out on a schedule) and conducting an in-depth interview. The latter involves a leap of imagination – a surrender to the perspective of your interviewee. As you listen you must try to see things from their point of view (no matter how uncomfortable or incredible that may be) and use your questions to elicit more. It is so easy to make assumptions about what is in a person's mind or what they are likely to say. The challenge is to set aside your worldview. Consider that a dog has one hundred times more olfactory receptors than we do; their first instinct is not to look or listen, but to smell. To understand a dog's behaviour, we need to consider things from their perspective.

Locking on to your interviewee in this way generates a sustained tension. From the moment the recorder goes on until the moment it goes off, you must concentrate completely. You cannot let your mind wander for a second – you must stay with your interviewee positively, encouraging them, supporting them, listening, and thus fuelling the interview. The opposite is disengagement.

Listening and at the same time giving shape and structure to the interview is underlined by time pressure. You must gauge how much time you can reasonably expect your interviewee to give, and remain alert to the first sign of tiredness.

Don't be afraid of silence

When we are apprehensive or nervous (as is often the case in an interview situation) we are inclined to gabble. Rather than risk an awkward pause in proceedings, it is tempting to race on to the next topic. A more confident interviewer will not shy away from silence and will instead afford the interviewee whatever time they need to compose themselves, reflect on the question, and offer additional reflections and insights if they so wish. With your eyes, facial expression, and body language you can communicate that you are interested and therefore listening intently, that you empathise with what the interviewee is telling you, and that you are keen to hear more.

Correct as necessary

An interview is not an examination. If you feel that you have misspoken or that you have framed a question clumsily, say so. If an interviewee's body language or eye contact (raised eyebrow, slight tensing, vacant expression) suggests that they do not understand the question or that they take exception to it, have the confidence to stop and say, 'Sorry, I'm not making myself clear. Let me rephrase that'. If you get the impression that the question is deemed irrelevant or somehow inappropriate and you do not understand why, then say so: 'Is that a misunderstanding on my part?' or 'Is that in your view an irrelevant or inappropriate question?' This demonstrates active listening, shows empathy and understanding, and (provided your interviewee is not mortally offended) may well serve a useful purpose. Affording them an opportunity to take your question apart is an effective way of eliciting their perspective.

When to interject

Questioning strategies range from the free-flow of 'truth-kick' encounter groups to the type of questionnaire we associate with market analysis. We have noted that the extent to which you shape your interview depends on the nature of your research (we return to this in Section 9). Studs Terkel claimed that he simply turned on the tape recorder and asked people to talk. Most researchers establish the broad parameters of the encounter, and within this allow the interviewee to set the pace. If your interviewee is shy or taciturn by nature you may find that, no matter how much time you leave for contemplative silence, you must have the next question ready. Interviewees with a public persona (for example, politicians) are often particularly skilled at saying as little as possible so as to avoid a faux-pas. They may deliver short, clipped responses, impatiently implying 'next question' or alternatively speak at length about issues that are peripheral to your research. This does not mean that you should despair of encouraging the person behind the persona to emerge.

Most interviewees take some time to 'warm up'. In the first few minutes of the interview they are forming an assessment of you, your knowledge of the topic, and your general demeanour. If your questions betray an inexcusable ignorance they may decide that the encounter is not worthwhile and fob you off with short and relatively shallow responses. If, on the other hand, they get the impression that you are genuine, sincere and respectful, they will most likely begin to relax and offer lengthier and more reflective responses. The most successful interviews then take on a life of their own. You need not even glance at your topics as you listen intently to the interviewee and pose follow-on questions based on what they tell you. When in doubt, listen.

It is sometimes hard to suppress your own views and opinions. Paradoxically, it is often easier to do this when you disagree with what is being said. You listen all the more intently in an attempt to understand the interviewee's perspective. If you agree wholeheartedly with what is being said it is often tempting to offer an even better or more colourful anecdote to underline and reinforce the point that they are making. There is nothing wrong with agreeing with your interviewee, but it is best to maintain a degree of professional detachment and to ensure that you do not take over. The important thing to remember is that you are an investigator and a recorder, not a co-respondent or a judge.

THE INVESTIGATOR INTERVIEW

My first experience of interviews was as a young police officer in the 1970s. These were promotion interviews and the style was quite confrontational. Over the years, research and reflection gave way to more sophisticated techniques. Consultants introduced us to competency-based models which, although imperfect, enabled less gruelling and ultimately more productive encounters.

I discovered early on – to my surprise – that I had a flair for investigator interviews. An international expert once told me that you either have it or you don't. To some extent that is true, but training can be of great assistance. It takes many forms. Perhaps the most effective type is mentoring. I learned much from observing experienced interviewers in action. They often found it difficult to explain to a group how they did what they did. You can tell people about the importance of gut instinct, understanding human nature, and adapting techniques and approaches in line with changing circumstances and moods, but it is much more effective to see those attributes applied in real life.

The best mentors freely admitted when things went wrong in interviews – they reflected on instances of 'tunnel vision', pinpointed tendencies towards a 'group mentality' or prejudice, and explained what they would like to have done differently. A good interviewer has no need to raise their voice; rather, they develop the ability to relate to a wide variety of people and to empathise with their circumstances.

In many ways our task is simple – we want to establish the facts of what happened. We do this by collecting all available evidence, testing its credibility, and corroborating it with evidence from other sources. Interviewing is a key element of that process, and in the course of the last forty and more years I have encountered every possible type of subject – those who are helpful, attention-seeking, talkative, and traumatised. Some have bashed their heads against the wall in an effort to prevent themselves from talking; others simply pick a spot and stare. Surprisingly often perpetrators have an urge to confess, and the interviewer needs to facilitate this. You try to establish some empathy with the suspect – where they are coming from and what makes them tick. This is where background research and exploratory interviews are very helpful. The information that you gather might seem peripheral or incidental, but such contextual information can later prove valuable. It all helps to build up a picture of the interviewee's world.

In trying to understand where a perpetrator is coming from you must keep an open mind. There can be no doubt that truth is stranger than fiction; some of the things that happen in relation to crimes and the events surrounding them are literally unimaginable. No matter how repulsed you might be by the crime, you need to set emotions to one side and try to see things from the perspective of the witness or the perpetrator. In some instances this almost enables them to forgive themselves – they can see an 'out'. That can, of course, be very difficult for victims, but it is often a necessary part of the process of establishing the facts of what happened.

The atmosphere within the interview room is very important. Over an extended period you seek to develop some kind of a rapport with the interviewee, and this can often be quite intense. At all costs you want to avoid bursting the bubble. Rather than turning on a light to enable note-taking to continue, you want to preserve the atmosphere. The last thing you want is a knock on the door to say that a meal is ready or a solicitor has arrived.

Professional discipline is key. You must have an acute understanding of the relevant legal framework, and you must avoid becoming emotionally and personally involved in a case. No matter how noble the cause or how frustrating the constraint, you cannot step outside the regulations. If you do it will come back to bite you, and when it does you will be on your own. If your misdemeanour was unintentional your organisation will support you, but if you wilfully go on a 'solo run' you cannot be supported. That discipline applies as much to a young police officer starting out as it does to a Superintendent. Decisions made in an interview for the most straightforward investigation could be subsequently reviewed by the Supreme Court. The ultimate horror is the conviction of an innocent person – this is a gross injustice for the wrongly accused, and the perpetrator is still at large.

Questioning strategies

Whether or not you decide to prepare topics in advance, it is generally best to begin with clear and open questions. The opposite – closed questions – can provoke monosyllabic answers.

Closed	Open
What was the name of your Primary School?	Can you tell me a bit about your Primary School?
Were you conscious of racial tensions?	To what extent were you conscious of racial tensions?
Did that have a negative effect on you?	In what ways did that affect you?
Have you ever visited Pakistan?	How did you feel about visiting Pakistan?
Did you consider emigrating?	What were your thoughts on emigration? Did you ever consider it?
Was your organisation satisfied with the deal?	What was the spectrum of opinion on the deal? What were the main arguments for and against?

The interviewee is your main focus, and we have thus suggested that it is best to suppress (or at least dilute) your personal views and reactions. For example, if an interviewee recounts with regret their reasons for believing that they were 'a terrible parent', do not express value-judgements such as: 'I don't believe you! That is horrific,' or 'That was clearly a bad move'. Rather, you might simply nod and say, 'What are your thoughts on that period, looking back on it now?' Listen to their story and help them to set the context and to explain how and why they acted as they did.

Of course, it is possible to combine open and closed questions. For example, you might begin by asking for the name of a Primary School and the years that your interviewee attended, and then proceed to ask an open question. Alternatively you can start off with general reflections and then ask for contextual details:

- Was this after you got married?
- This was before you were conscripted?
- Can you remember roughly what year that was?

If you find that your question has provoked a short answer and you want to know more, ask for illustrations and examples. For example:

Q How did you reconcile your various responsibilities – to the Church, to victims, to society?

A It varied quite a bit. You were sometimes pulled and stretched in different directions. There were many challenges and crises of conscience over the years. [Pause].

Q Can you think of any telling examples?

Asking for detail will solicit colour, context and meaning:

Q What was the distinctive contribution of your organisation?

A Our main role was to provide humanitarian aid – to get the relief in, to identify those most in need, and to distribute it fairly and proportionately. That is easier said than done, and some of our officers were better at managing the process than others.

Q Are there particular individuals or events that stand out?

Another technique is to ask your interviewee to address a question in a number of different ways. For example, your prompt might read:

Q The closing of the factory clearly had a major impact on the town. What were the effects a) short-term b) long-term?

Or:

Q How did this affect a) you personally b) your family c) the wider community?

Linking questions

In introducing new topics, try to refer back to what was said earlier. This shows that you are listening and that you value what you are being told. It also makes sense to mould and adapt your questions to suit your interviewee's particular expertise and experience.

More probing questions

Open-ended questions are designed to encourage your interviewee to give reflective and wide-ranging responses. Depending on the interviewee and the nature of your investigation, you might want to intersperse them with more direct and challenging questions. Common sense dictates that you should first establish rapport and understanding and avoid questions that could possibly alarm or offend. If appropriate, you can then introduce more probing questions. More often than not interviewees will respond by saying, 'That's a really interesting question. I hadn't thought of it like that before.' If they have been interviewed a number of times before, a slightly provocative question will make them sit up and reflect afresh on their experiences and perspectives.

Examples might include:

- Was this the most important thing ever to happen to you?
- To what extent have you changed? Do you still recognise that young woman?
- Has Christianity failed in its Swedish mission?
- To what extent are people in this part of the world hard-wired for sectarianism?
- Is the class struggle still relevant?
- What is your organisation's greatest a) triumph b) failure?
- Do you have any personal regrets?

If you decide to pose direct and challenging questions it is important to deliver them in plain language and with confidence. If you race through the question and then shrink under the table, your interviewee is much more likely to consider it inappropriate. On the other hand, if you speak clearly and respectfully hold their gaze, they are much more likely to offer a frank and unabashed response. There are some questions that need nerve to ask. Often the hindrance in such instances is in your mind, rather than in that of the interviewee. Be brave.

Encouragement

We all respond well to praise and encouragement. Be sure to let your interviewee know that what they are telling you is of value and interest. Before moving on to the next question, say, 'That is very interesting. Could you develop it?' or 'I hadn't thought of it like that, but it makes perfect sense now that you say it.' No matter how reassuring your stance, shy interviewees will pause frequently to say, 'Is any of this of any interest? Are you sure this is the kind of thing that you want?' As noted, in these instances you will need to spell out how and why their recollections are of value.

Departing from the script

It is vitally important that you leave both the back and the side doors open. You should enter all interviews in a spirit of open and honest enquiry, ready to set aside all prior assumptions and knowledge of the topic. Your background research demonstrates respect for your interviewee, shows that you are serious, and will help you to pose reasonably well-informed questions. However, it should never exclude or constrict the unknown. New perspectives revealed by interviewees may well shift both the parameters and the direction of your research project. It could be disastrous and short-sighted prescriptively to stick to your questions and thus close off a theme, an interest, or indeed voices hitherto overlooked. Use your outline flexibly and imaginatively and remain open to unexpected twists.

Auto-pilots

We have considered reluctant interviewees. At the other extreme you will encounter those who need no encouragement whatsoever. If what they are telling you is relevant and interesting, this need not pose a problem. However, if it is a stream of consciousness of minimal relevance to your research you may need to intervene. A successful interview needs traction and guidance. Once rapport has been established and the interview is up and running, you should try to keep rambling to a minimum and probe obscurities and evasions where appropriate. If your interviewee continues to waffle or shows a determination to be evasive after a series of gentle but firm interjections, you may need to write the interview off and diplomatically bring it to a close.

Those in the public gaze understandably have an eye to the present and to the potentially damaging consequences of a word out of place. Others are fixated by the future and in particular by thoughts of their legacy. This generally means that they have given some considerable thought to their role in past events and to their personal narrative. We all do this to some extent. Memories are inevitably filtered and coloured by subsequent experience and knowledge. The process of rationalising our past and current lives is part of the essence of being. As we discuss in Section 9, some researchers are indeed more interested in the *way* in which interviewees remember than *what* they remember.

On one occasion we recorded a man who spoke in pre-composed paragraphs, as though dictating a neat transcript. It was clear that he had given much thought to his role in past events and to how he wished this to be remembered. This was self-justification by rote. Unlike a probing investigative journalist, our primary objective was not to dismantle this construction. We came to record his story; it was his truth, and he was entitled to present it as he wished. However, once the pre-prepared account had been released, we were able to introduce questions that respectfully considered his experience from a range of different angles. He then proceeded to offer more spontaneous and unfiltered reflections.

Wearing your knowledge lightly

We have noted that some interviewees will test you in the early part of an interview. They will want to know that you have taken the time and trouble to find out a little bit about them and your research topic. Others may find this intimidating, disconcerting, and (if they place a high value on privacy) even offensive. You need to judge how and when to demonstrate your background knowledge. Your grasp of the relevant issues, events and terminology will be apparent from the questions that you put (Was this before the Anglo–French

Economic Agreement? Had you stepped down by this stage? In what ways did the '57 embargo affect your trade?). We have noted that apparent ignorance can on occasion be an asset: it may surprise, goad and encourage the interviewee to put you and the record straight. They will most likely be delighted to learn that this is your first visit to their part of the world, and they will welcome an opportunity to put their place on the map. As noted in the Introduction, most people love nothing more than to talk about themselves. As long as you show a respectful desire to learn and have done your best to prepare for the interview, interviewees will generally look kindly on any gaps in your knowledge or understanding.

In a very early interview one of us was at great pains to demonstrate that 'homework' had been completed. The ensuing transcript was in many ways an example of how not to do it. The interview was dominated by long-winded questions that precluded the unique information that the interviewee had to offer. Thankfully the forgiving victim agreed to a second interview and all was not lost. The following extract from the original interview illustrates the point.

EXTRACT FROM TRANSCRIPT

BD: I was explaining to you earlier, before we began, that I'm interested in those riots in 1938. I hadn't even heard of them before I started this project, but I spent the last few months going through the local papers for this whole period and it's amazing the impact that they had. It seems to have brought the town to a standstill for weeks on end, and a few people I've spoken to said that it poisoned the atmosphere for years and years afterwards. The bunting seems to have been the main bone of contention. I suppose in earlier years the top end of the town had been more or less ignored, but the election of George Farraway in '37 changed all that.

RMcL: Well you have all that, now what was the next thing.

BD: Well the next thing really was the War and the effect that it had on community relations. John O'Reilly was explaining that the fact that the marching ceased for the duration of the War was important. I did read a bit about that in one of these books that I brought – do you see here, they're explaining what the situation was like in Belfast. It was interesting too about the refugees. I suppose there wasn't the same opportunity for travel in those days, so this must have been quite a novelty really.

RMcL: It was a novelty, I suppose. Of course I was away for most of the War so my memory of all of that wouldn't be so good.

What can go wrong?

The best way to avoid or mitigate potentially negative outcomes is to anticipate them. Here we set out issues that can arise and how you might deal with them.

Your interviewee breaks down

If you plan to discuss an emotive topic then you will most likely have considered this prospect. We have often been surprised to learn that an interviewee is speaking for the first time about their recollections of a particular event or episode – that they have never discussed the matter with their wives, partners or close friends. In these instances they cannot know how they will react to the unfolding of memories. As noted in Section 1, it is important to remember that the most innocent question could indirectly provoke an upsetting memory.

Crying is a very human reaction. Most individuals are not ashamed to shed a few tears and thus to acknowledge grief or sadness; others may feel a little embarrassed and laugh off the process. For some, however, it can be mortifying to break down in front of a relative stranger.

As an interviewer it is important that you recognise the reaction: do not proceed as if nothing has happened. If necessary, gently interject to say, 'I can see that this is upsetting for you', and then give the interviewee whatever time they need to compose themselves. You must then judge whether the tears are indicative of a passing emotion or the cause of some considerable upset. Ask the interviewee if they would like to break for ten minutes. (A short interval is often productive. It enables both parties to relax and further develop rapport, and is generally preferable to rescheduling.) If you feel that the interviewee is too upset – or that resuming the interview is likely to distress them – you should nonetheless offer to come back at a later date. You might then follow up with a phone-call to thank them for making the time to see you and to enquire how they are. If they live alone and you feel that they have been deeply troubled, try to make contact with a relative or friend and explain what has happened. In extremis – if you are truly concerned for the safety and/or well-being of the interviewee – seek professional advice and assistance.

Your interviewee gets angry

Your interviewee may express a wide range of emotions in the course of an interview (happiness, sadness, pain, sorrow, regret, frustration, nostalgia, bitterness, etc.). While it quite in order for an interviewee to recall the past with anger, it is quite another matter for them to direct anger at you. It is highly unlikely to arise but if your interviews raise issues of cultural, religious, social or political sensitivity, an interviewee might take exception to the manner in which you pose a question, or they may decide to channel their anger about the issues under investigation towards you. Whatever their motive, you need to remove yourself from such a situation as quickly as possible. If it is safe to do so, allow the interviewee to vent their anger and then apologise for unintentionally upsetting them. Try not to take any abuse personally, and suggest that you get back in touch when you have both had a chance to reflect on what has gone wrong and why. On reflection, if you feel that something that you said or did was out of order or unintentionally insensitive, then follow up with a letter of apology. If appropriate (and if you think there is any possibility of success) you might want to ask whether or not they would consider offering you a second chance. On the other hand, if you feel that the reaction was unwarranted, unreasonable and unjustified, then send a note indicating your regret that the interview was the cause of upset and confirming what you plan to do with the recording. If the interviewee has not already indicated their preference you will need to negotiate this with them. Assuming that any copyright accruing to them has not been assigned to you in writing, you should agree to destroy the recording if that is the interviewee's clearly stated preference.

You get upset

You are not a passive participant. In discussing the ways in which you can show respect for your interviewees, we suggested that there are certain categories of people that you may not be able to interview effectively – whether because of your background, your publicly stated views, or because you cannot agree to abide by the necessary terms and conditions (dress-code, language etc.). It is also possible that what an interview relates may affect you in an unforeseen way. It may trigger an emotional memory, or the interviewee may make a statement that upsets you because of something that has happened to you in the past or because it offends your values or beliefs.

Within reason, try to suppress your feelings and focus intently on the interviewee's story. If it all gets too much, pause the interview and (if appropriate) explain to the interviewee that you need a moment to compose yourself. If you feel able to resume the interview, do so, but do not be afraid to call a halt to proceedings if you need a break. Even the most straightforward interviews can be intense and emotionally draining. Without betraying any confidences, it is often helpful to 'debrief' with a colleague or friend.

Bruising encounters

Only once in the course of hundreds of research interviewees has one of our interviewers been reduced to tears. This was the result of a pre-planned attack on the part of an interviewee. A formal letter of invitation was issued, and as requested, a schedule of topics was sent out several weeks in advance.

The interviewer made the necessary arrangements (domestic and professional) to travel for half a day, stay overnight and then arrive at the interviewee's office at the agreed time.

What transpired was tantamount to an ambush. Although he had ample opportunity to raise any objections to the project title or to the topics selected for discussion with the project director, this interviewee quite deliberately waited until the interviewer arrived to launch into a full-scale angry attack. This was in effect a party political rant, but it was delivered with such venom and rage that the interviewer was completely taken aback and became quite upset. There was no question of conducting an interview and the precious resources expended both on preparation and logistics were simply wasted.

This was, moreover, a bruising and completely unjustified attack on the part of a rude, angry and obnoxious individual. It was also an abuse of power. Thankfully this has been an isolated incident. Over the years many interviewees have raised questions and concerns about topics, terminology and protocols – as indeed is their right. Although sometimes robust, these exchanges have always been respectful, courteous and professional.

One is company

Interjections by relatives and friends are often welcome. They might help to put an interviewee at ease or to jog their memory. If, on the other hand, the third party diminishes the interviewee or effectively takes over, the effects can be disastrous. One memorable example of the latter took place during a review of an elderly interviewee's transcript. As we went through it line by line the lady concerned became more and more confident about the value of her recollections. And then her daughter arrived. As she leafed through the pages she sighed. 'Oh mother, your grammar is atrocious.' The confidence-building collapsed, and the interview was ultimately lost.

On another occasion an interviewee asked if an old friend (with similar experiences) could sit in on his interview. This interview proceeded well until one of them went to the toilet. The second interviewee then proceeded to dismantle and disagree with almost everything his friend had said. In some ways this was a useful corrective, but your primary task as an interviewer is not to arbitrate between conflicting versions of the past (this can come later). It is also difficult simultaneously to develop a rapport with two people, and there can be a tendency towards conformity and generalisation. (Luck can turn against you. If it does, write off what has been lost and take comfort in the fact that it all balances out.)

In our experience, one to one interviews are generally preferable – but there may well be situations when it is either obligatory or preferable to interview two or more people together (for example, if you are doing research on ballroom dancing or tennis duos). Two interviewees can sometimes spark each other off to great effect; in these instances, one plus one yields more than two. If you are interviewing more than one person you will need to pay attention to sound quality (ensure that each wears a microphone). You should also take every opportunity to identify the interviewee ('From what you're saying, Jane, I understand that [...] Now let me know put a similar question to you, John'). This is particularly important if a) both interviewees have similar accents, and/or b) you plan to outsource the transcription of the interview.

You lose an interview

If you take care to record and promptly upload your interview recording, it is highly unlikely that you will ever lose an interview. However, if an interview has failed to record (due to a technical or human error) or you somehow manage subsequently to delete it, you must inform the interviewee. They have given the account in good faith and have a right to know what has happened. Depending on the individual and the circumstances you may be given a second chance. It may also be possible to retrieve something from your interview notes and from memory. You can then at least send this to the interviewee as the basis for a fresh recording. If you are working with, or on behalf of, another individual or organisation you should immediately report the incident and seek advice as to how best to proceed.

You discover that a third party has accessed confidential material

It is important, first, to consider what constitutes confidential material. To a large extent this is dictated by the interviewee. A seemingly innocent anecdote may be confidential to the interviewee, and its unexpected disclosure could cause considerable embarrassment. All information, therefore, should be considered confidential until you have explicit permission to release it; this includes factual details such as age, address, education, work experience etc. (The nature of private and sensitive data is set out more fully in the context of data protection legislation.)

If you have taken all reasonable steps to protect and safeguard your recordings and transcripts, it is highly unlikely that the issue of unauthorised access should arise. However, if the confidentiality of your material is compromised for some reason (oversight, carelessness, theft), you must immediately report the issue to an appropriate senior. This might be the project director or – if you are working independently – a trusted colleague or friend. If you fear that the accounts have been accessed unlawfully you will need to report the matter to the police. If you know who has accessed the material (for example, staff in your department or organisation), seek permission to issue a notification alerting people to the confidentiality of the material and plead with them to respect the wishes and rights of the interviewee in question. At any rate you must let the interviewee know that a potential breach of security has arisen, and inform them of the steps that you have taken to mitigate the damage. You must then conduct a thorough review of your protocols and procedures and take action to minimise the chance of the same thing ever happening again.

You betray a confidence

If you knowingly or unknowingly betray a confidence (which could include divulging the very fact that an interview has taken place), you must immediately take steps to repair or mitigate the damage. This might involve contacting the individual(s) concerned to explain that you should not have divulged this information and alerting them to the potential repercussions for you, your colleagues, and your employer should this become public knowledge. Depending on the scale and nature of the likely repercussions, you should consider the steps outlined above in the context of a breach of security by a third party.

Knowing when to stop

It is easy to lose track of time if you are fully engaged in listening. If you have travelled some distance to see an interviewee and the information that they are relaying is particularly useful, it is very tempting to 'milk it'. However, you should resist the temptation to stretch an interviewee beyond reasonable limits (especially if they are elderly or infirm). Look out for signs of tiredness, hunger or unease. It is much better for you to bring the encounter to a confident conclusion than to exhaust your interviewee and possibly irritate their family or colleagues. Each interview is a performance, and you have responsibility for ending it. Our interviews have typically fallen in the one to two hour range. On occasion they have extended to two or even three hours, but these were exceptional in-depth encounters. It is generally a good idea to offer a short break after forty-five minutes or so, and then let your interviewee decide if they want to press on or reschedule a follow-up meeting. Once you have signalled that the end is in sight, for example by saying something like 'I have just a few closing questions', you may find that the interviewee is quite happy to keep going for another half hour. It is important to leave time to bring the interview to a satisfactory close.

Once the recording has ceased you will need time to pack away your equipment and notes (rather than having to scramble them into your bag as the interviewee realises the time and politely ejects you from the building). You will most likely want to take a photograph, and you must ensure that the interviewee signs the consent form. (If they indicate that they want to wait until they have seen a transcript you must abide by their wishes, but it is best to have it signed at the end of the interview if possible.) Finally, you will want to take some time to thank your interviewee and to recap on what will happen to the recording.

Once you have returned to base and have uploaded your recordings, it is vitally important that you take the time to write to your interviewee and to any facilitators to thank them for their kindness. You should also make a separate note of your reflections: what worked and what did not, what you wanted to ask but didn't, how successful the interview was overall, and what you will do differently next time.

I have been interviewed at least fifty times across a range of print, radio, and television media, mostly in relation to my imprisonment (prison experience generally, recollections of a hunger strike and protest that I participated in, and the educational and creative writing projects that I helped to develop). My inclination is to accept interview requests as I feel that I have a personal responsibility to articulate my perspective and that of my community. The act of 'telling' (in the interview) is for me a political act, even if it concerns my personal experience. As the feminist quote goes, 'the personal is political'.

Interviewers have for the most part been students, anxious to draw on 'primary sources' for their dissertations. Having conducted interviews for my own graduate research I feel obliged to facilitate them wherever possible – even when they are seeking information that could easily be gleaned from publicly available sources. It is undoubtedly more interesting to be interviewed by a researcher who, equipped with background knowledge, wants to dig deeper and take a new angle on existing accounts. This leads to a much more reflexive discussion.

It is immediately clear to me whether or not an interviewer is interested in their topic (rather than being sent to complete a task on behalf of another). You also quickly get a sense of whether they want to *learn* or *take* from you. They don't necessarily have to be an expert in the field of study, but at the very least I think that an interviewer should demonstrate an interest in the research topic and show a willingness to respond to advice on areas that might be explored or others who could be interviewed. While I am always willing to help students, I am occasionally surprised by those who assume that I would like to do their research for them.

Regardless of how much you try to ignore it, gender often makes a difference in the interviewer-interviewee relationship. A lot also depends on the interviewer's ability to identify and tease out contradictions and variations across the accounts that they collect. The best interview experience I had was with a BBC journalist who travelled from London to see me. I took exception to her choice of terminology and asked her to reflect on this, and to her credit she did just that. She returned a few days later and we engaged in a totally different, critical and reflective interview.

A transcript is always welcome. It lets you see in black and white what you have said, and ideally there will be some indication of which elements of your account will be used. I have rarely needed to change my account, but on occasion I have discovered that the interviewer had misinterpreted what I said or that I had not elaborated sufficiently on a particular topic.

My worst interview experience was with a senior academic. It was abundantly clear within minutes that he was determined to capture a 'sound bite' to fit the narrative of his forthcoming book. Throughout the interview he returned to the same topic seeking the same line. Needless to say, my contribution did not feature in the finished work. Thankfully this was an exception, although I have detected a certain element of manipulation in interviews for television documentaries: if what you have to say does not fit with the predetermined thrust of the programme, your contribution is discarded or mere snippets are used. I do understand the pressure to condense volumes of information and to shape things into a concise and appealing programme, but it is worth cautioning would-be interviewees that, although you have given up an hour or two of your time, only a fraction of what you say (if that) may be used. Only the finished product will reveal whether or not the interviewer/director set out with an agenda, or if they dealt with the topic in an even-handed, sensitive, and investigative manner. I resolve this dilemma by reminding myself that if I don't participate, I can't argue afterwards that my story or that of my community has not been told.

Live or recorded interviews for radio or television programmes (as distinct from documentaries) are quite different. You are fully aware that your comments may be broadcast, and you are therefore much more 'on the spot'. My fear is always that I will say the wrong thing without any opportunity to explain myself thereafter. Thankfully this rarely happens, but you should consider carefully the nature of the programme. It you are invited to be interviewed by a presenter who is known for trying to whip up emotions among the audience rather than trying to tease out your story, then you need to prepare accordingly. On the other hand, if the presenter has a reputation for trying to develop an interesting, informative exchange then my experience is that this is a worthwhile opportunity – although it may still be a little nerve-wracking. It is all down to the interviewer to ensure that they get best out of you.

However, there *is* an issue with telling your own story repeatedly. I discovered this during one of the significant anniversaries of the hunger strike when I gave a series of interviews (including public 'question and answer' forums). I found that reliving the experience of the hunger strike on a regular basis did eventually have an emotional and psychological effect. I think that there is also a need to reflect on the story you tell, and not to simply become the story. I also find it interesting to reflect on the ways in which the narrative of those events has evolved. In addition to speaking about the specifics of the situation, I am increasingly interested in other elements of the experience – the wider personal and human dimension, as opposed to the big political issues of the time.

Mock interviews

Trial interviews work particularly well in training, as they provide an opportunity to practice skills, gain confidence in operating recording equipment, and at the same time to think about how it feels to be interviewed: both interviewer and interviewee can subsequently report back, providing valuable feedback for discussion.

In advanced training we have engaged professional actors to play the part of the interviewee. We sketch a number of scenarios and then select interviewers at random from within the group. Those selected are given ten minutes to prepare for the interview (brainstorm possible questions, assemble all necessary equipment and paperwork and compose themselves). The interview is then conducted live in front of the wider group. The actors are assigned roles in advance (and they dress accordingly), but since they do not know what questions the interviewer will put, they must improvise: their skills and discipline ensure that the scenarios are realistic and that any giddiness is kept at bay.

These sessions always provoke intense analysis. It can be quite a challenge to greet a complete stranger, introduce a project, establish a rapport, operate the equipment, develop questions, bring the interview to a close, take a photograph and have a consent form signed. Our 'interviewees' tend to be unusually difficult. For this reason it is best to reserve these sessions for advanced training with those who have mastered the basic skills and have come to enjoy the interview process.

The object is not to scare them off, but rather to help them think about how they might overcome challenges. In crafting scenarios we aim to:

* Introduce students to a wide variety of interviewees (young, old, confident, shy, talkative, evasive, formal, prickly, co-operative)
* Confront them with unforeseen challenges (the arrival of a third party, mild objection to a question, a noisy interruption) and test their response
* Develop confidence in performing under pressure (answering questions and establishing rapport while assembling equipment and paperwork)
* Let them see how enjoyable an interview can be.

Some examples are set out below.

Project on emigration

Brief for interviewer:

You live in a rural community. Having recently retired, you are looking forward to documenting the history of emigration from your local area. Your budget is modest: at your own expense you have purchased a solid-state digital recorder, but you plan to transcribe the interviews in your own good time. Your ultimate ambition is to publish a book, but at this point you are not sure how feasible that will be (adapt consent form accordingly).

At a recent festival you were introduced to Rose Harkenrider who emigrated from your village in 1942. She is due to return to New York later next week, but she has gladly agreed to be interviewed at her hotel. You have arranged to meet her in the lobby at twelve noon.

You have been told by a neighbour that her story is fascinating: three people died on the liner on which she travelled to New York, she had a bizarre experience at Ellis Island, and she ended up sleeping rough. She eventually worked her way through night-school and qualified as a primary school teacher.

Your objective is to record this lady's story. You want also to know what your local area was like when she was growing up, why she decided to emigrate, how she got the fare together, and whether family and friends had gone before her. You would also be interested to hear about her experience as an emigrant in New York.

Brief for Rose Harkenrider:

You are a busy lady. The noisy and distracting hotel lobby is not the ideal location for an interview, but it is up to the interviewer to find an alternative. You are keen to talk about your recent holiday, your beautiful children and a gorgeous new grandchild. It will be a challenge for the interviewer to bring the conversation around to the topics that he/she really wants to cover. You will also interject with questions that he/she may find distracting. You have another appointment scheduled, and – glancing at your watch – you will bring the interview to a close just as your story begins to unfold.

Project on local factory

Brief for interviewer

Your community group has just received a small grant to conduct a 'story-telling' project, documenting the history of Wilkinson's shirt factory. It was built in 1921 and came to play a central role in the economic life of your city. During the Second World War the then flat roof was used as an anti-aircraft gun site as it overlooked a ship repair yard. The building has since been converted into modern apartments.

You and another community worker have been tasked with collecting a representative sample of thirty interviews. You must include both employers and employees and a suitably diverse range of Protestants and Catholics, men and women. You want also to include some interviews with members of the local community.

You are committed to producing a short book documenting the history of the factory.

Through your contacts in the trades union movement you have managed to interview five former shop stewards. Your colleague lives near a retired factory manager, and through his contacts he has interviewed all of the surviving factory managers. Aside from the shop stewards, you have not yet captured the stories of the men and women who worked on the factory floor.

Sandra Morgan has reluctantly agreed to participate. She is quite daunted by the prospect of an interview. She has agreed to see you at her house this afternoon. Her husband plays bingo on a Wednesday afternoon and it is important that he is not present. He might object to her participation.

Brief for Sandra Morgan

You are a spritely woman in your late seventies. You left school at fourteen and went straight to work in the shirt factory. You got married in 1959 and gave up work when your first child was born. You went back to work when the youngest started school.

You view your interviewer with a degree of suspicion. You wonder what you could possibly contribute to a project like this. You would like to know who else has agreed to contribute and what they have said. You want to emphasise that you don't have any interest in history or politics, and that you like to keep yourself to yourself. You don't want the neighbours talking. You are very wary of the recorder. Assuming the interviewer succeeds in allaying your fears and putting you at ease, you might relax and open up as you begin to talk about the good times. You loved the factory – the buzz, the fun, the excitement. Although you handed most of your pay over to your mother for the first several years, it gave you great independence. You quite enjoy the interview in the end, but you are nonetheless reluctant to sign the consent form. You are also quite embarrassed about getting your photograph taken.

Project on holocaust

Brief for interviewer

You are in your final year at university and want to write a dissertation based on interviews with Holocaust survivors. You have held an exploratory meeting with a Survivors' Group. Lucille Eichengreen has subsequently agreed to participate.

You know that she arrived in Auschwitz in August 1944 and was later transferred to the work camp, Dessauerufer, in October 1944. She found refuge in Ireland following the liberation in 1945. You are scheduled to interview her at her home.

Brief for Lucille Eichengreen

You were born in 1925 in Hamburg, Germany. Your father was arrested for the first time in October 1938, but he returned in the spring of 1939. He was taken again the day the War broke out, but this time only his ashes were returned. At the age of sixteen you were deported to the Lódz Ghetto in Poland, where you remained for nearly four years. You arrived in Auschwitz in August 1944; you were later transferred to Dessauerufer in October 1944. From there you were transported to the camp in Neungamme. You made the journey to Bergen-Belsen and finally you were liberated in April 1945. In 1946 you were brought to Ireland by Dr Ralph Durrow, and you were later adopted by an Irish Jewish family.

You are physically frail but your memory is excellent. You are a shy person who has never before spoken to a stranger about these traumatic events. You are worried about upsetting your grandchildren, and you want to know where the dissertation will be stored and what will happen to your recording. You would like to know that you can withdraw the interview if you change your mind. This is a subject that arouses deep emotions: your memories are painful, and some are literally unspeakable. You are co-operative but you speak very slowly and quietly. You might take exception to some of the terms adopted by the interviewee. You do not want your photograph to be taken.

6

SPECIAL CARE

We have emphasised that all interviews must be approached and handled with care, with due regard for the unexpected. If you plan to research a topic of particular social, political or organisational sensitivity you will need to take additional steps to safeguard your interviewees and your research materials.

Embargo

If there is any possibility that the information you intend to gather could libel, damage or perhaps even endanger your interviewee or third parties, then you will need to consider an embargo.

Some interviewers offer partial restriction or closure, giving the interviewee an opportunity to ring-fence those elements that are not suitable for immediate release. Others offer staged access so that some interviews are immediately available and others are restricted.

While it makes sense to consult your interviewees before settling the terms and conditions of access, you should acknowledge that you have primary responsibility for any consequences arising from the interview, including the safety of all concerned. It is quite possible that an interviewee will be happy (and perhaps even insistent) that their full account should reach the widest audience as soon as possible, but you must explain that you are strictly bound by ethical and legal guidelines. Many interviewees are happy for their account to be made public after their demise. While this arrangement protects the interviewee from any potential repercussions, it has no regard for third parties; you must agree an embargo that balances the interests of the interviewee and those of all other relevant parties. In our experience, the thirty-year rule governing access to many government documents in the UK, Ireland, Australia and many other countries provides a useful model.

It is important that your interviewees understand that there is no such thing as a cast-iron guarantee of closure. Your consent form should stipulate that the material will remain closed to public access unless required to be disclosed by law or by the court or other authority of a competent jurisdiction. Risks most commonly arise in relation to crimes that have not been processed and fully determined by the relevant criminal justice system, or information that is likely to breach legislation such as official secrets or prevention of terrorism acts. It must be stipulated in writing on your consent form that you cannot offer an absolute guarantee of confidentiality. The archive clause might read something like this:

PRESERVATION IN ARCHIVES

I/we (named individuals/institutions) wish to preserve your interview material by depositing copies under embargo at archives in X and Y. This means that, aside from the uses set out above, the accounts will not be released for consultation until 1 January Z, unless required to be disclosed by law or order of a court or other authority of competent jurisdiction. By signing this waiver you agree to copies of your interview material being deposited.

Signed   ....

Date   ....

Witnessed by   ....

Ensuring confidentiality in collecting, processing and storing your research materials (negotiating with archives etc.) is costly and time-consuming, and it also brings with it a considerable burden of responsibility. As with any assurance you offer to your interviewees, you must be able to stand over it. You should thus think carefully about the resources and commitment (both short- and long-term) that may be necessary to give weight to an embargo.

Disadvantages of an embargo

- It is a significant sacrifice for other scholars who might wish to draw upon, benefit from, or challenge your work. In principle you should not restrict access to your interviews unless it is absolutely necessary.
- It might draw undue attention to the interviews, sensationalising and dramatising the content and encouraging requests for access under the terms of freedom of information or data protection legislation.
- It is costly and time-consuming to enforce, bringing obligations that may extend for many years beyond the recording of the interviews.

Advantages of an embargo

- It may well be a necessary evil: the only way in which reluctant interviewees will agree to participate.
- Interviewees are more likely to speak frankly and for history, rather than with the constraint of duty to others in mind, or the politics and pressing concerns of the moment. This can create a momentum of revelation and truth that would be impossible to achieve in conventional academic research or journalism.
- It is a considerable reassurance for interviewees to know that your mutual goal is to preserve material for future generations rather than to serve any short-term or selfish motive.

If you do decide to introduce an embargo, you must give careful consideration to security issues.

- Take legal advice on the wording of your consent forms and the implications of data protection and freedom of information legislation for your project.
- Encrypt (to the appropriate standard) all desktops or laptops containing interview files and related confidential databases and supporting documentation. Never use 'shared access' computers.
- Use encrypted external drives (expansion drives/USB keys) for the transfer of audio files and for back-up.
- Avoid the use of email for the transfer of interview files unless it is absolutely necessary. If files must be sent electronically, ensure that they are suitably encrypted, immediately uploaded, and deleted from the relevant transfer folders. Do not allow confidential data to sit in cyberspace.
- Do not use internet-based solutions for data storage.
- Ensure that any smartphones that may contain biographical data (for example, interviewee contact details) and/or emails relating to interview processes and procedures are encrypted.
- Use a secure (ideally heavy, fire-safe) cabinet to store your encrypted expansion drives and any documentation relating to the interviews, pending transfer to an appropriate archive.
- Arrange permanently to delete and physically destroy all hard drives that ever held interview-related files, save those copies that are deposited within an appropriately secure archive. Bear in mind that when you 'delete' a file from a computer drive you simply remove it from immediate view, and it can quite easily be retrieved. If you are using an encrypted USB key and you want to delete files to enable you to reuse it, you should reformat the key after deleting your files. A fail-safe way to decommission a hard-drive is to remove it from the computer, take a hammer to it and then immerse the parts in a bowl of water. The process should be photographed and witnessed.

An alternative is to have a reputable commercial company carry out the task for you. They will usually certify the process.

• Devise a written contract (setting out your agreement to adhere to established security guidelines and to abide by obligations under the terms of the relevant legislation) to be signed by all relevant members of staff, including outside contractors. An example is set out below.

SECURITY MEMO [PROJECT NAME]   DATE

The *[Project Name]* team is committed to the security of all project data processed and stored both electronically and in hardcopy format.
The following policy guidelines must be adhered to by all project staff to ensure that project data is protected at all times.

1. Desktops used to store confidential interview data must be encrypted using a full disk encryption product (industry standard).

2. All computers (desktops/laptops/tablets) used to store or process confidential data must have the hard disks permanently deleted or destroyed once the data has been transferred to an appropriate archive (or if the machine becomes obsolete).

3. All external devices used to store or process confidential data, e.g. USB devices, external hard drives etc., must be encrypted.

   Note: Where confidential data has been processed and is no longer needed it should be permanently deleted/shredded.

4. All smartphones, tablets or other mobile devices used to temporarily store or process project data must have a strong password at start-up and after a few minutes of inactivity.

5. All postal communications containing sensitive project data must be sent by signed for/registered post.

6. If semi-confidential documents must be sent by email they should be password protected. Further, they must immediately be deleted from *all* relevant mailboxes once the confidential document has been uploaded to the appropriate encrypted drive. Timing for sending/receiving to be arranged in advance by telephone. Confirmation of deletion should then be issued by means of a separate email and/or text message.

7. All passwords used to log into computers or mobile devices, or to access encrypted/password protected files must be good 'strong' passwords and should not be words that you would find in a dictionary.

   Bad password examples include: password (too obvious), red (too short), marysmith (names are obvious).

   Good password examples include: wiHufh8h5% (ten characters, not a dictionary word, includes letters, numbers, a capital letter and a symbol).

8. Passwords must not be stored with the device that they protect.

   E.g. a login password for a computer should not be written on a post-it note stuck on the computer. This is important, because it would invalidate the encryption on a computer if it were lost or stolen since anyone seeing the password could log into the computer. However, you must ensure that another team member is aware of your password.

9. Passwords used to encrypt documents that are sent by email must not be sent in the email also. They should be communicated via a different medium, e.g. by phone or text message.

10. Passwords used to protect data in this project must be new passwords. Do not reuse passwords from your email, college, Facebook, Gmail etc.

11. All external media hardcopies of confidential data (printed documents, hard drives etc.) must be stored in a fireproof safe which is for the sole use of this project and which cannot be accessed by any individuals not related to the project.

    Note: the key or pincode for the safe should not be stored/written down in the same room or elsewhere in the vicinity of the safe. However, another team member must be made aware of its location.

12. No confidential data related to this study should ever be stored on an internet server or in internet accessible document storage, even for backup purposes.

13. Data must be backed up to an encrypted external hard drive which is stored in a fireproof security cabinet.

    This is the responsibility of X, Y and Z. Part-time employees involved in this project must not make backups or copies of any project data without the express permission of the Project Directors.

Signed:

Date:

It is vital periodically to review security measures. Few projects operate within a static environment (there will most likely be some changes in personnel and in the location of staff during the lifetime of the research). Technology is evolving rapidly and you need to be vigilant about the security implications of new software and equipment.

As with all security reviews, you must consider both the likelihood of a breach and the potential repercussions. If the likelihood of a breach of security is minimal but the potential damage is great, then on balance you must proceed to introduce all proportionate measures to safeguard the confidentiality of your material.

Implementing an embargo demands that you assume almost total control over the interview recording. It is common practice to afford interviewees the right to review and if necessary to edit their accounts. Unless you are satisfied that the interviewee fully understands the need to protect the confidentiality of the interview collection as a whole, agrees to abide by established security protocols and is capable of so doing, it would be most inadvisable to issue a transcript or a copy of the recording. Even if the interviewee does fully understand the need to abide by such conditions, they could die before you have an opportunity to retrieve the script, or they may return it only after making a copy for inclusion in their personal papers. Upon their death, their next of kin may then consign the script to the wastepaper basket, or leave it on the morning train. Even if the content of this account was utterly banal, the 'leak' could still do considerable damage to the wider project and to your ability to convince other interviewees that your embargo is meaningful.

If the interviewee is anxious to review their script and you are reasonably satisfied that they understand the implications of any breach of security for the wider project, you should ask if they intend to retain a copy. Then, if necessary, request that they affix to the transcript a top-copy memo (such as the one set out below) for the benefit of their successors.

- This transcript is part of a wider collection on [nature of research].
- It was created as part of [name of project], led by [name(s) of project director(s)] of [name of institution/organisation].
- These interviews were conducted rigorous standards of ethics and accuracy.
- The interview was recorded and then transcribed by a confidential secretary.
- A waiver was developed in consultation with legal counsel.
- That waiver (setting out the conditions under which the interview was recorded and, subject to these, assigning copyright in the interview to X) was signed by the interviewee and returned to X.
- In consultation with IT security and legal experts, all reasonable steps have been taken to ensure the complete confidentiality of this material in processing.
- A cardinal concern was the protection of all interviewees (including their personal security) and the preservation of these interviews from any possibility of journalistic or other exploitation.
- Upon completion of the recording, transcribing and editing process, this collection will be deposited at X, an archive capable of securely storing and preserving the material, whatever the technological developments of the coming decades.
- It will not be made available for public access until [date].
- These are the clearly expressed conditions under which the interviewee agreed to contribute to this project.
- If an interviewee wishes to edit their account, we have agreed where possible to provide them with a copy of the script.
- We ask that they return a marked-up copy to us, and we will then edit the script before archiving it with the original voice recording.
- We are conscious that some individual interviewees may wish to retain a copy of their script for inclusion in their personal papers.
- Therefore, we ask that family members, or any persons who might access such a copy now or in the future, should be made aware of the facts and procedures outlined above, and that they do not in any way breach the confidentiality, copyright, or integrity of the heritage collection as a whole.

7

SHIFTING FOCUS

Almost everything you have read thus far is relevant to audio-visual interviews. The skills necessary to master this medium are really an extension of those that we employ in audio work. Hearing and seeing provoke different kinds of emotional responses in the viewer or listener. Thinking about your audience – how and what you want to communicate to them – will help determine whether you need to employ picture as well as sound.

The moving image

Capturing sound and vision has never been easier. Rapid advances in technology have generated an increasingly accessible range of recording equipment, and the synergies between the creators of audio and audio-visual recordings are many. Both have the desire and drive to document new stories and perspectives. Film-making is a growing and varied profession, and it is now more possible than ever to develop creative partnerships and thus open up new opportunities for the dissemination of your stories.

There are two clear routes into the audio-visual world. If you plan to 'go it alone' you will need to undergo some training. You will play a dual role as interviewer and camera operator. This need not be daunting; you are already familiar with using a microphone and recorder, and learning to use a camera to record image as well as sound is simply the next step. The core additional skills relate to framing and shot sizes.

The second route leads to the kind of documentary you are accustomed to seeing on television or in the cinema. For this purpose you will most likely need to engage the assistance of a crew (or at least an assistant). In this section we review the pros and cons of each approach. However, before we do so, let's consider the advantages of the audio-visual format.

Integrating picture and sound

A still camera captures an image. The viewer sees what they see. However, the audio-visual camera goes well beyond 'superficial' appearances. For example, it records how a person:

- walks and talks (their gait and general demeanour)
- sits in their seat (slouching, on edge, upright, awkward, relaxed)
- moves or holds their hands, gestures or gesticulates
- listens (intently, closely, distractedly, looking away, looking at the camera, closing eyes)
- speaks (softly, loudly, gently, clearly, with accent, carefully, slowly, aggressively, fluently, with difficulty)
- moves their eyes (twinkles, winks, blinks a tear, stares, looks away)
- uses body language (frowns, raises eyebrow, folded arms, shoulders back, tenses)
- how they visibly respond to a question (laughs, relaxes, expresses shock, horror, anguish, suspicion, pain, delight, frustration, confusion, approval).

We can visualise the person being interviewed and the location in which the encounter takes place – with all the added and implied meaning that this brings. Set out below are some examples of the kinds of interview location you see on television and what they might denote.

Interview location	Implied or inferred meaning
Garage or fire station	A practical person
Classroom	A student or teacher
Study with lots of books	A scholar, someone cerebral
Kitchen	A family person, a parent or home-maker
Office	A business person or professional
Living room	A homely person
Inside a car, in a car park	A person who has something to hide
Dressing room	A performer
On stage	Someone in the public eye
Lecture theatre	An expert in their field
TV studio	A public figure

Developing an awareness of all that the camera captures is key. An inexperienced operator will record material that detracts rather than adds meaning. The visual information recorded should be there for a reason. Showing a badge or insignia on someone's jacket (for example, denoting allegiance to a particular football team) may well be something that you (or they) want to communicate. In other instances it may pigeonhole an individual and unhelpfully distract from what they are saying. This kind of issue does not arise with an audio interview.

Whether film or not

- Will visual information help my audience to understand what is being said?
- Will it add meaning and depth?
- Is it necessary for the outputs I have in mind?

Images can be powerfully seductive. By integrating visual and recorded material you will exponentially increase the opportunities and outputs for your research. Multiple platforms exist on the web (ebooks, blogs, websites like YouTube and Vimeo, online resources and so forth). Audio and visual material can also be 'decoupled', creating opportunities for podcasts and vodcasts. Learning how to work with picture and sound, together and separately, will enable you to reach a much wider audience, including those who are not inclined to read books, those who find it easier to digest audio-visual information, and the ever-widening cyber-community.

It is also possible to produce a documentary film, even on a shoe-string budget. Most researchers will want to start with a pilot. They will shoot their own footage and then use this to apply for funding to develop the material to suit a particular documentary strand or television series. This is not always necessary. *Tarnation* (2003, 88mins, USA) documents the life of a young man, Jonathan Caouette, and his mentally ill mother. It was compiled from hours of old family videos and interviews; the total cost of production was $218. Caouette (the filmmaker and focus of the film) edited the material using simple iMovie software (now pre-installed on most Apple computers). The film was awarded Best Documentary Film by the National Society of Film Critics in America in 2004, and was screened in international film festivals to critical acclaim. (Funding was secured to cover the copyright clearance costs of music and clips from old films, thus enabling the film to be screened in multiple jurisdictions). It is interesting to note that Caouette casually collected recorded material over a period of years, in both audio and video form. He filmed on various low-grade video cameras; recorded sound on ghetto-blasters or whatever else he could get his hands on, and had scant regard throughout for established codes and conventions. He became a professional by making mistakes and learning from them. Since 2003, when *Tarnation* was cut, technology has advanced at a seemingly relentless pace. The demographic of internet users has also changed dramatically, to include preschool children using iPads and those in their nineties surveying online census data. The tools of the filmmaking trade are now so readily available that the only things standing in the way of successful production are operational skills and imagination.

There are many ways to integrate still and moving images into your working practice. They can enhance your recordings and help to bring the subject to life. In this section we examine the basic requirements for working in this field. The pace of change is such that we can only highlight the current possibilities. Your basic skills and creativity will help you to identify and exploit new technology as it becomes available.

Extras

An added advantage of the audio-visual medium is the capacity to layer your interview with 'extras'. Alongside the edited interview, a researcher can feature discarded sections and a post-interview exchange with the interviewee. They can film their own reflections on the assignment: what aspects of the work they found most challenging, what they would like to have done differently, what worked, what did not, and why.

Other 'interactive' possibilities

The internet has transformed the way we communicate, and in turn the nature of research, scholarship and dissemination. More and more source material is now available to a worldwide online community. Audio-visual recordings were once confined to special interest DVDs, websites or blogs. These days, however, many art galleries and museums offer excellent spaces for exhibiting your work. Conventional radio and television are no longer the only ports of call for your documentary: you might want to consider semi-closed platforms to test your product, allowing it to snowball around interested parties. The internet thus enables you to reach a variety of specialist audiences that will give your work a proper review as opposed to relying on the somewhat superficial response of a major production company. If you decide to publish your film online you can also provide links to a range of relevant resources – online books or articles, databases or statistical resources.

What are the limitations?

Using a camera as opposed to a discreet recorder and microphone is undoubtedly more intrusive (especially if you come with an entourage). The introduction of lights, powder to dampen the shine on a forehead and studio-like set-ups can all inhibit your interviewee. They may feel under pressure to 'perform' and fail to deliver 'real' responses. This may prove counter-productive: you come equipped with the tools necessary to capture more, but those same tools cause your interviewee to communicate less. You should thus reflect carefully on the type of interview you want to conduct, the extent to which your interviewee is likely to be 'camera-shy', and your end product.

In the past the main disadvantages of using a camera were the cost and bulk of the kit. However, the advent of nanotechnology has opened the way to smaller and lighter cameras. Equipment that was once the preserve of video professionals is now within reach of the average consumer. This does not guarantee top quality image or sound, but it does open the door. With skilful handling and a basic understanding of shot sizes, framing and editing software, you can produce watchable films, incorporating interviews, cutaways, still images of documents, voice-over narration, sound tracks and on-screen text in whatever combination you choose.

Key considerations include:

*   Lighting: natural light is preferable, so you may have to ask your interviewee to sit in a particular position in order to make best use of available light.
*   Background sound or interference: it can be difficult to cut or edit the talking head without the interviewee appearing to 'jump' in the frame (known as a 'jump cut').
*   Expense: although they are increasingly affordable, adding a video camera to your kit will cost. If you cannot afford a model capable of delivering the desired output you may ultimately be disappointed.
*   Compatibility: if you plan to use your smart phone or tablet as a back-up, it is vital that you test the quality beforehand to check that the output matches that of the main camera.
*   Assistance: depending on your level of expertise and level of filming you anticipate, you may need to engage a crew (they will most likely prefer to use their own kit and you need to budget accordingly).
*   Expertise: be realistic about your abilities. Are you prepared to put in the necessary time to make effective use of the equipment that you have bought or hired, learn how to edit to the appropriate level; and process the raw material - sub-editing, adding titles, subtitles, voice-over, music etc.? If not, you will have to either lower your expectations or raise your budget.

Thinking ahead

As with audio interviews the key to success is forward planning, and you must then check and recheck as you go. Inattention to detail can potentially blow weeks of preparation and a once-in-a-lifetime opportunity.

The table below sets out some key questions that you should ask yourself before deciding to film. This list is by no means exhaustive but it will help to get you started.

Location

Issue	Action
Do you need to book the venue you are using for your interview in advance? Is a fee required?	Book well in advance for popular locations and discounts. Tip: hotel meeting rooms are much cheaper at off-peak times.
Are you filming in an outdoor location or on private grounds using a tripod?	You may need a filming permit from the local council or written permission from the landowner. Tip: always carry the relevant paperwork with you.
Do you plan to interview people on the street (vox pops) as well as more carefully selected individuals?	You must have a consent form for all who 'talk' to the camera. In most instances passers-by will not need to sign a consent form, but see the section on Legalities for exceptions.
Are you familiar with the location? What health and safety issues might arise? (For example, do you plan to film in a factory with dangerous equipment, or in a tumble-down cottage in a rural setting?)	Bring extension leads to avoid trailing or stretched wires. Avoid naked flames (a hotel kitchen, bonfire, open hearth), pools of water or damp, moist conditions, and extremes of temperature. These may affect the mechanics of the recorder. Tip: before heading out 'on location' consider taking a first aid course.
Is the location a 'hostile environment' (for example, a conflict zone, the scene of a natural disaster, or even a problematic housing estate or interface area)? What kind of insurance do you have?	Are you personally insured against injury? Is your equipment insured? To what extent are third parties insured? Can you make contact with other people who have recently been there? Tip: always carry your ID, a copy of your passport, details of your country's Embassy, your health insurance details, and contact details for local hospitals.
Have you done a recce or recon of the location?	You should check the following: • Which direction does the natural light come from? Will you need extra lighting? • What are the best places to position the interviewee and the camera? • Where are the electrical sockets – in the walls or the floors? • What are the acoustics like? (Avoid echoey rooms) • What will you use as a backdrop for your interviewee? • Will you need any props (for example, a book shelf, flowers, musical instruments? In other words, do you need to 'dress the set'?)

Kit

Issue	Action
Do you have sufficient recording material (for example, tapes or SD cards)?	Always bring twice or three times more than you think you might need.
Have you tested all of your recording equipment?	Make sure that you check all of your equipment including your batteries and microphone several days before the interview in case you need to replace a specialist item such as tapes or SD cards.
Have you tested the microphone with your headphones on prior to the interview? Have you established the best place to position the mic?	Is a lapel mic more appropriate than a shotgun or boom? Practice with a friend beforehand.
Have you brought your electrical power charger as well as spare batteries for your camera? Do you know how much shooting time you have for each battery? Do you have an extension lead (if any of your equipment is not battery operated)?	You should have a check list in your camera-bag which you go through in advance of the shoot. (Camera batteries usually need to be charged for a long time, preferably overnight.) The basic list should include: • Camera (see camera types) • Camera mains lead • Camera batteries (charged) • Several clean tapes or SD cards (check to ensure that the SD cards are blank) • Separate mics (lapel, shotgun and boom if necessary) • Batteries for the mics, if required • Two tripods – one large, one small • Headphones • Back up recorder – smartphone or equivalent.
Have you checked the settings on your camera?	If you are on auto-setting, the focus may not stay still. It will constantly zoom in and out trying to fix focus. This is very annoying to look at and you may have problems editing such takes.

The shoot

Issue	Action
Is the camera powered up?	Check if the power light is on.
If using a tripod, is the camera securely fastened on the head? Is it level?	Test to ensure that it will not fall off if nudged.
If setting the camera on the table, do you need to raise the height in order to get a better eye-line or a better frame?	Shots that look up or down on the subject can make the interviewee appear either too dominant or too submissive. They are also unflattering to the face. Avoid this by using either a small table tripod or some books to raise the height of the camera.
Have you checked the white balance?	If you are filming both indoors and out, you will need to adjust the settings on your camera: tungsten light (indoor/yellowish) and daylight (outdoor/blueish). If the camera settings are on manual, this needs to be changed on the camera as you move from interior to exterior.
Do you plan to use a mid-shot framing throughout?	If so, check the focus and make sure that your interviewee cannot move too far out of the frame – for example, do not put them on a chair that swings around or that moves on wheels.
Have you checked that the microphone is working? Have you rechecked with a set of headphones?	This is essential! If your mic is not functioning properly your efforts will come to nothing. Check and check again. Some mics have their own battery – check it in advance. Some mics take power from the camera (phantom power) when they are plugged in; again, check in advance.
Have you conducted a sound test?	Once the mic is in position ask your interviewee to speak. Ask them a simple question like what they had for breakfast. Meanwhile check the record level either on your audio recorder or camera. Voice should peak at about 12dB. Tip: record some room atmosphere (silence). This may be useful for your edit.

The edit

Issue	Action
Have you access to a laptop or computer with a basic editing package pre-installed?	The most common are: • iMovie (Apple computers – basic) • Movie Maker (PC – basic) • Avid (professional) • Final Cut Express or Pro (both) • Premiere (both)
Have you got the correct cables to link your camera or audio device to the computer you are using?	Usually this will be a firewire cable or a USB cable, depending on the camera or computer you are using. Check this when you buy or hire your camera.
Have you kept a log of all the material shot? Do you plan to transcribe your interviews?	There can be no short-cuts here. The more information you have regarding your material, the easier the edit will be. Observe and log all relevant material. Transcribe interviews in full if you can.
How will you approach the edit?	Don't get caught up in minutiae early on. Make a very rough cut to begin with; this can all be tidied up once you decide on the focus of your film.
Will you let others review your work in progress?	A fresh eye is always helpful. When you are immersed in recording and editing, it is easy to lose track of clarity. What seems self-explanatory to you may actually be quite confusing for a viewer. The more feedback you can get at different points in your edit, the better.
Will you add sound and music to your film?	If you want to add sound you must observe the following rules: • Always make sure you have secured the necessary permission • Do not edit **to** the music. Everything should be cut with the native sound attached. Once you are happy that everything is in the right place then you can identify which part(s) might benefit from some music. • Generally it is not a good idea to whitewash your film with music – even if it is your favourite song. It can distract from what is being said on screen, even when dimmed to a low level.

Contingency

Things do not always go according to plan. Some things are beyond our control, and with the best will in the world, we can all make mistakes.

Case study

You have scheduled an interview with Davey, a gardener. You want to film him in the grounds of the castle that he has tended all his life. On the day you arrive it is pouring with rain. What do you do?

Your first concern must be the well-being of your interviewee. You cannot ask him to stand out in the rain for the sake of the backdrop, no matter how crucial you consider it to be. You then cast your mind back to your pre-interview visit to the location. On that occasion you noticed a large greenhouse. It is well lit and full of little pots of seedlings. Davey often works there, so it is an appropriate backdrop for the interview. It is not your first choice; you are concerned about the sound of heavy rain hitting the windows and the possibility of glare from the windows if the sun comes out. However, you mitigate your sound concerns by opting for a lapel microphone which will hone in on Davey's voice, keeping the rain firmly in the background. If it stops you may step outside and adjust your set-up accordingly. You check to ensure that Davey is happy with your plan.

Remember:

Your interviewee's time is precious. If you are too demanding or unreasonable, you might achieve your ideal set-up but you will not get the best from your interviewee. Within reason you should try to accommodate their needs, preferences and schedule.

Outputs

As mentioned at the beginning of this section, much will be dictated by your desired end products. Set out below is a list of potential outputs and the process required to produce them. We start with the most basic (and the lowest budget) and progress to more complicated operations (where higher levels of funding and a professional film crew may be required). This table will help you to decide what level of audio-visual equipment and expertise you need.

Output A	Blogs, websites, lectures
Plan	Who do you need to interview? How can you contact them? What kind of shots do you need for your blog, website, lecture? (Talking head, medium close-up?) List the various options in a table.
Shoot	For a talking head interview with one shot size only, probably a medium close-up (MCU), you will require, audio and video recordings on a digital camera with a separate microphone (do not use the onboard microphone on your camera).
Crew	One person can perform both the role of interviewer and camera/sound person. They will also be responsible for issuing consent forms and getting them signed.
Kit required	One small video camera, a lapel mic or a shotgun mic. Tripod optional. One back-up smartphone to record sounds and images, if necessary.
Editing	Most laptops/computers have pre-installed editing software packages. You will digitise the footage and bring it into a timeline. You can then trim the clip to cut out the voice of the interviewer and/or any other non-essential information, add a simple title, and check the sound levels to ensure that the recording is audible. Once you are happy that the clip is ready you can export it from the timeline as a mov or mpeg file. You can then upload it to your blog, social networking page or website or insert it into your presentation (talk, lecture etc.)

Output B	Blogs, single channel video platforms such as YouTube or Vimeo
Plan	Set out what you want to achieve and who you would like to interview (both essential and desirable). What kind of shots are required (close up (CU), medium close up (MCU), cutaways etc.)? Again, compile a series of lists/tables.
Shoot	A talking head interview. One shot size only (MCU). For this output you will additionally shoot cutaways, close-ups on hands, close-ups on the face, as well as shots that detail the interview space (ornaments on mantelpiece, old photographs on piano, books on shelves). You might also want an establishing shot of the interviewee in their chair, and perhaps an exterior shot. This can all be done post-interview (schedule permitting). It is usually easier to pinpoint images after an interviewee has shared their story.
Crew	One person performs the role of both interviewer and camera/sound person (with an assistant to help if possible). The interviewer/assistant will issue consent forms and ensure that they are signed.
Kit required	One small video camera to record audio and video, a separate microphone (not the onboard camera microphone) – a lapel mic or a shotgun mic is recommended. Again, a tripod is optional.

Editing	A laptop or computer with a simple editing software package. As above, you will digitise the footage, bring it into a timeline and trim the clip to cut out the voice of the interviewer and/or any other non-essential information. The editing work will be more detailed. First, cut the interview into sections. As you listen to each section, review a list of the footage that you have and jot down where it might fit in. For example, as your interviewee talks about their early years you will be reminded of the old photograph of them as a child. As they go on to speak about the student protests of 1968 you will recall the anti-Vietnam war poster you captured on the way out. Once the interview is inter-cut with the relevant visual material you will have what looks like a short documentary piece. You can add a simple title if required. When the sequence is complete, export it from the timeline as a mov or mpeg file. As before, you can then upload it to your blog, social networking page or website, or insert it into a slideshow for a talk, lecture or presentation. It can also be uploaded to a platform for single screen documentaries or to a single interest discussion room or forum for feedback.

Output C	Film for Broadcast or Cinema
Note	The parameters shift considerably when you introduce a team. The key to success is communication. If you plan to work with a camera operator you must familiarise yourself with the terminology used to describe the shots you require and for what purpose you require them (see page 117 for more details). In turn, they need to understand the nuances of what you want to capture. If they have not been told that your interviewee is very proud of the fact that one of the boys he trained went on to play professional football, they may overlook a photograph of a local football team. If they do not understand that you are particularly interested in the religious formation of the individual, they may not pause to capture the full range of theological works on his bookshelf.
Plan	Present an outline shot list to the crew – the kinds of shots you think you will need while the interview is being conducted. Listen to their advice – they will have a lot of experience of framing, choosing appropriate shot sizes and so on. Issue checklists to tick off during the day.
Shoot	You will need to shoot some or all of the following: • **Testimony:** Recording of information or perspectives offered by a witness, expert or other participant. This may involve a talking head interview, or simply recorded voice. You will normally shoot several different frame sizes – establishing shot, mid shot, close-up etc.

	• **Overheard Exchange:** This is the recording of seemingly spontaneous dialogue between two or more participants engaged in conversation. As above, you will also shoot 'cutaways' – for example, close-ups of hands and faces, additional shots that detail the space itself (ornaments, photographs, memorabilia, books), or a long shot of the interviewee in their chair in the space. Again, an exterior shot taken outside the building in which the interview takes place may be desirable. You might also want to record the grounds, any interesting details on the building or its gates, nearby streets and shops or, if in the countryside a rural scene. As noted in the section above, it is often easier to capture these post-interview when you have a clearer idea of the relevant themes.
Crew	Two or more people who will perform the role of interviewer, camera operator and lighting director. You may also require a separate sound recordist. You or an assistant will be responsible for organising consent forms and getting them signed.
Kit required	If you budgeted to hire a professional crew, they will most likely come with their own kit (do not ask someone to operate a camera they are not familiar with or have never used before). It is vitally important that you discuss in advance how the filmed material will be presented to you. Will you receive transferred digital files, or, if the footage is shot on tape, will you ask for the tape to be converted to digital files? Either way, you need to ensure that you will have ready access to the recorded material. You also might want a copy of the original tapes for your own archive. If some of the material that you capture is confidential, you may insist that the crew's copy is destroyed. All of this must be established before you set out.
Editing	Depending on your budget and your expertise, you will either make a rough cut of the material yourself or you will work with a professional editor. Performing a rough cut (using a personal laptop or computer, as above) can save much time in the professional editing room and will therefore save you money. To save further time later on, keep a list of the clips that you definitely want to use in the final version and store them in a separate folder on an external hard drive. It is important to be as methodical as possible, naming all folders and files so that you can easily identify material when working with your professional editor on the 'online' or final edit. Your edit does not need to be perfect. It is designed simply to block out roughly what is in and what is out, and how the material might be slung together. This will give you much more control over the final output because you will have reviewed the footage in its entirety and will have a good sense of the narrative – the beginning, the middle and the end.

Working with a professional editor	Once you are satisfied with your rough cut you can deliver all the clips on a hard drive (retain a copy for your own reference/back-up). If you have edited using Final Cut and your online editor also uses this software, you can save your whole project to an external hard drive. The editor will then work with you to fine-tune the edits, sounds, credits and titles. A word of caution, however, – an editor may miss the finer points of subtlety within the interview. They may also favour image over substance, and thus remove a shaky shot even though what is being said is critically important. It is thus vital that you, as producer, should communicate clearly what you want to retain or discard.
	You should also give some thought to sound. Bring copies of your preferred tracks and discuss with the editor where they might be placed to achieve the right balance of voice/background track. (See Legalities for details of how to secure permission to use sound recordings.) The editor can then advise you on the finer points of the edit, perhaps suggesting a more sophisticated title or credit sequence. This helps to achieve a professional and polished finish.
	Once the film is finished to your satisfaction, the editor will export it from the timeline either as a mov or mpeg file or in another format to your specification, and will produce a version for DVD. This will be your master copy to be reproduced for distribution or projection proposes.
	Screening: Depending on who has funded your project, there may be restrictions on where and when it can be screened. Some funders will insist on a private screening before the film can be shown publicly. Others will require a premiere screening at a particular film festival, or if it has been funded by a television company, they will most likely require that it is first screened on their preferred channel. It is crucial that you review the terms of your funding contract before uploading your film to any internet platform (including social media sites). However, it may be possible to create a trailer for your film in order to promote it. It might also be possible to adapt your material for educational purposes such as talks or presentations – but always check in advance.

Adhering to a legal and ethical code

A: Interviewees/Participants

As with audio interviews, you will need to establish that your interviewees agree to be interviewed and that they understand the purpose for which the interview is being conducted (by whom, for whom and sponsored by whom). It is important to spell out that you intend to edit their contribution (without distortion or misrepresentation). Explain that observations will be edited, primarily for the purposes of length. Film interviewees are rarely offered editorial control over the final cut, so they must trust you to represent what they say with integrity and honesty.

As noted above, a consent form is also required for anyone who speaks to the camera (even in passing, as in a vox pop). If you are filming in a sensitive area (such as a hospital corridor, a law court, a betting office or a gay club) you will need to complete additional paperwork to cover and protect individuals who may be visible in the background. If in doubt, take advice. It is better to overdo the consent forms that to discover that vital footage has been compromised by an uncleared 'extra'.

In view of the varied (and ever-changing) platforms available for dissemination it is best to create an all-embracing waiver. A television broadcast may seem highly unlikely at the inception of your project, but it is impossible to know how your work might snowball. If your interviewee is uneasy about the proposed level of exposure, try to ascertain what outputs they would be comfortable with and amend your waiver accordingly. Be sure to establish clearly in writing the specific restrictions that they want to introduce. If they have had a change of heart with regard to audio-visual exposure, ask if they would consider letting you use the audio recording (either alone, with a different camera angle so that the interviewee's face is not shown, or to support an anonymous voiceover).

B: Location releases

You will need permission to shoot anywhere other than in a public street or in a property that you own yourself. If you want to shoot on public transport networks (trains, buses, or underground systems) or in public places (schools, hospitals, clubs, bars etc.), allow plenty of time for your filming request to be processed. Many locations will require that you put up signs to say that you are filming, and will ask that you get written permission from anyone (customer, client, passer-by) who appears in your film. You must keep and carry with you a signed letter outlining your permission to film in a particular location.

C: Other releases

You also need to consider the specific clearances and permissions necessary to include supporting material. Again, it is much better to seek permission at the outset than to hang whole sections of your material around a soundtrack or image, only to discover that it is not possible to use it. Whether or not there is payment involved, you need to inform the owner of your intention to use their material and get their permission in writing.

For many educational projects you will be able to avail yourself of a publicly available (free-to-use) copyright licence with relaxed restrictions, such as a Creative Commons License. This will enable you to use certain copyright works for educational purposes. These public copyright licences enable certain copyright protected works to be distributed, shared and enhanced by others. For example, some musicians and artists only allow non-commercial use of their work under the terms of these licences. There are many variations of agreement and you need to check carefully whether or not the desired piece of work falls into this category. It is always best to check with the artist, publisher and/or distributor. Reference works such as the Filmmakers' Yearbook or the Writers' and Artists' Yearbook may help with contact details.

It is worth noting that some online music websites sell background music at a relatively low cost. You might also consider asking a musician to compose something for you in return for a credit (and the promotion of their talent). Even if the musician is a close friend and you both clearly understand the terms and conditions of the arrangement, you should still create and sign a written agreement. In general, avoid filming copyrighted works, such as paintings or photographs, and well-known visual branding (such as McDonalds) unless it is essential to the story. Also, quite aside from permissions, remember that your product should contain at least 80 to 90 per cent original material.

Here is an outline of the types of issues/material that require clearance.

What you need to clear	How you need to clear it
People and places	Interview and location release forms
Music (whether from CD/cassette/record, downloaded from the web, or live recording – in public or private setting)	Clearance from the proprietor/copyright holder (artist and/or publisher)
Documentary material: books, articles, poems etc.	Clearance from proprietor/copyright holder (publisher and/or author)
Websites, blogs or any material from the web	Clearance from proprietor/copyright holder (author and/or host)
Advertisements – for example, shots of billboards or posters	Clearance from the proprietor/copyright holder (company for whom the advertisement has been compiled and/or advertising company)
Privately-owned film clips, photographs and memorabilia	Proprietor/copyright holder and/or head of the family
News footage	Proprietor/copyright holder (most likely the news-gathering organisation)
Newspaper clippings	Proprietor/copyright holder (newspaper owner and if necessary the author)

Additional legal considerations

As with any research, it is important to remember that filming certain groups will require additional safeguards. For example:

- Interviews featuring minors (individuals who are under eighteen). Here you will require the written permission of a parent or guardian. You will need to conceal the faces of any children for whom permission to film has not been granted. The written permission of the appropriate school or local authority may also be required.
- As with audio recordings, you cannot accept material about crimes that have not been processed and fully determined in the courts of the relevant jurisdictions. For example, you must take every care to ensure that you do not record material that could be defamatory or prejudice due process.
- Take particular care with stories that are controversial or contentious, and think very carefully before publishing material that could lead to you or your interviewees being threatened or harmed.

Sample documentary release form

Name and address of researcher/producer (or letterhead of production company)
Name and address of contributor:
Title of the documentary/research project (may be a working title)

I agree to be interviewed and to the inclusion of my contribution in the above documentary. The nature of the documentary has been explained to me. I understand that my contribution will be edited and that there is no guarantee that my contribution will appear in the final film. I agree that my contribution may be used to publicise the documentary.

I have agreed to accept _____ in return for the use of my contribution. This fee is payable on completion of the interview.

I understand that this documentary (or sequences from it) may be distributed in *any* medium in any part of the world.

My contribution has, to the best of my knowledge, been truthful and honest. I have told the truth and have not deliberately sought to conceal any relevant facts from the makers of this film.

Signed:
Date:

Sample location release form

From: Name and address of company/individual
To: Name and address of proprietor
Date:

Dear (Proprietor)

Re: Name of film (the 'Film')

This letter is to confirm that you (the proprietor) have granted permission for us to film at _____, hereafter referred to as the 'Property', from [start time] to [finish time] on [date]. We will set up between the hours of [x and y] and will do everything in our power to vacate the premises by [x].

It is therefore agreed as follows:

1. That the personnel, props, equipment and vehicles employed on our production are permitted to access the Property for the purpose of setting up and filming at the agreed dates and times.
2. We may return to the Property at a later date if principal photography and recording is not completed within this period.
3. We have notified you of the scenes which are to be shot on or around the Property and you confirm and agree that you consent to the filming of these scenes.
4. We are entitled to incorporate all films, photographs and recordings, whether audio or audio-visual, made in or about the Property in the Film as we may require in accordance with our sole discretion.
5. We shall not make any structural or decorative alterations to the Property without your prior consent. In the event that we do want to make alterations to a part of the Property and in the event that you agree, when our filming is completed we shall reinstate that part of the Property to its condition prior to those alterations.
6. In consideration of the rights granted in this letter we will pay you the sum of [£amount] on [date].
7. You agree to indemnify us and to keep us fully indemnified from and against all actions, proceedings, costs, claims, damages and demands, however arising, in respect of any actual or alleged breach or non-performance by you of any or all of your undertakings, warranties and obligations under this agreement.
8. This agreement shall be governed by and construed in accordance with the law of [England and Wales] and subject to the jurisdiction of the [English] Courts.

Please signify your acceptance of the above terms by signing the enclosed copy of this agreement and returning it to us.

Yours sincerely,

Signed....................................

Resources: the camera

Recording format	Some popular brands and models	
Mini DV Tapes	Panasonic DVX100, Sony, PD150, PD170 Z1, A1 Canon XL1, H1 (under 1-2k)	
	Pros	**Cons**
	These video cameras have traditionally been popular with semi-professionals. They are now available second-hand at very competitive prices as they record on tape (as opposed to digital cards).	Finding focus in low light conditions can be challenging because the viewfinders tend to be quite small.
	They are generally easy to operate. As always, study the manual closely to ensure that you are familiar with the settings and you can find your way around the camera with confidence.	In order to transfer footage for editing you must link to your computer via a firewire cable/ port.
	A good choice for longer interviews.	The recordings take real time to digitise (if you shoot one hour of footage, it will take at least one hour to digitise).
	The tapes offer an hour (63 minutes) of running time. They are affordable and available to purchase in most camera shops.	There are concerns about the long-term viability of video tape, but if you are careful about storage (using a water/ fire/damp-proof box) it should not degrade in the short-term.

Recording format	Some popular brands and models	
SD Card	Sony EX3 and similar cameras models by JVC and Panasonic (under 3k)	
	Pros	**Cons**
	This is now the most popular professional camera; there are few downsides to working with this type of model.	More expensive than the models mentioned above. It is unlikely that you will commence shooting on such a camera, but you might consider making the investment and then working with a hired camera operator until you are sufficiently confident to operate independently.
	You can connect external microphones via SLR cables and thus achieve excellent sound quality.	Some operational training required for optimum benefit.

This type of camera is broadcast standard. They are commonly used by documentary teams working for large TV corporations such as the BBC.	Somewhat heavier than the cameras mentioned above, so a tripod is essential.
	You must remember to bring extra memory cards as these may not be available to purchase locally.

Recording format	*Some popular brands and models*	
SD Card	DSLR Canon 500D, EOS M, etc. *(under 1k)*	
	Pros	**Cons**
	The latest models of these cameras offer cinema quality images at affordable prices. For example, you can obtain shallow depth of field for a fraction of what this would cost to shoot on high-end professional cameras.	While the level of image quality provided is necessary for screenings in large cinemas and art galleries, it may be lost on the average internet audience.
	Recordings are stored on SD cards which you can easily upload to your computer.	It is important to note that these cameras are designed primarily for still photography; audio facilities are often the poor relation.
	Light, compact and easily portable.	They do not have onboard audio limiters, so it is best to record your audio on a separate recording device and sync it with your video in the editing programme later. This can be fiddly and time-consuming.
		These cameras are generally quite compact but you will need a tripod to keep it steady. Shaky pictures are a problem when it comes to the edit.
		Again, with SD cards you must always carry spares because it can be hard to gauge exactly how much space you will need.
		You will also have to save the original footage onto a separate hard drive if you want to reuse your SD card. Careful handling and storage is essential.

		Lastly – and this is probably the main reason why many documentary makers do not tend to use these models as a primary recording device – these cameras have a limited shooting time before they overheat and shut off (somewhere in the region of ten to fifteen minutes). This is obviously problematic for longer interviews.

Recording format	*Some popular brands and models*	
SIM or MINI SIM Card	iPads, tablets, smartphones such as iPhones, Samsung, Nokia etc. (c£500)	
	Pros	**Cons**
	Smartphones and tablets are fast becoming an everyday commodity, and most have inbuilt HD cameras.	One of the main challenges is keeping the device steady; arms tend to get tired after just a few minutes.
	Light and discreet.	You can prop the device on a table, but it is difficult to avoid distorting your filming angle. The best solution is to purchase a mount or stand which attaches directly to the device and enables you to use a tripod.
	Performs best in an acoustically sound environment with good lighting conditions.	The recorded sound will not be top-quality. Ideally you should connect an external microphone. If this is not possible, take care to avoid obstructing the onboard microphone with your hand or an object.
		Motion distortion is another challenge, so keep panning to a minimum. The rolling shutter on these inbuilt video cameras does not deal well with movement.
		Also bear in mind that the focal range on your camera is likely to be limited, so take care when shooting close-up or use the macro function.

		The touch exposure controls tend to be sensitive, so watch out for bright lights behind your subject. Allow a few moments for the camera to adjust to a new scene or lighting condition before asking your question.
		Battery power can drain quickly – always bring a mains adaptor. Before setting out check the storage capacity on your device and tailor your expectations accordingly.

Resources: the editing kit

Choosing an editing system can be daunting. If possible seek the advice of an expert, reminding them that you are a beginner and you want something that is reasonably easy to navigate. You should also be realistic in terms of your budget, and think carefully about what you actually need in order to achieve the desired result. Most computers now have basic editing software pre-installed. Begin by practicing with this. Read around the subject, take online tutorials, and if you can, attend a course. If your interviews involve travel it will make sense to invest in a laptop or tablet instead of/in addition to a desktop computer. (You can also record directly onto these devices if required.) Below is a list of basic kit (as of mid-2013). These specs are subject to continuous change, and you must keep a close eye on the necessary processing power and hard drive space. Complex graphics demand considerable processing speed; if you plan to use a simple title, a moderate processor will suffice.

	Mac or PC	Software	Specifications
Basic	iMac (21.5" or 27" screen)	iMovie	Intel Core i5, 500GB, Mac OS X M Lion
Intermediate/ Advanced	Mac (separate screen size of your choosing)	Final Cut Studio/Final Cut Express	Intel Xeon Core, 1TB, OS X Lion
Intermediate/ Advanced	PC (separate screen size of your choosing)	Premiere or Final Cut	8GB RAM, 1TB
Intermediate/ Advanced	MacBook Pro 15"or 17" screen (laptop)	iMovie or Final Cut Express	Intel Core i7, 750GB hard drive

Notes on hiring a self-equipped crew

- Check the specifications of their standard kit in advance.
- Discuss lighting: how much space does their equipment occupy?
- How quickly does the equipment heat up?
- What kind of tripod do they plan to use?

As noted, communication is key. Meet your crew in advance to discuss the desired shooting style, footage and the ultimate objectives of the exercise. Inform them about any potential sensitivities (personal, local, social, religious or political). If you need to involve a series of crews, ensure that all members are given an equally comprehensive brief. (For example, you may wish to integrate old video or super eight footage, restored photographs, reel-to-reel tape recordings, diagrams or maps, or combine footage that has been shot by colleagues working in a different country.)

If your film has multiple components you should prepare a brief for all participants. This should include the core elements of what film sponsors refer to as a 'treatment' (in essence, your proposal). It should detail all that is necessary to create the desired film – from the interviewees' names and locations through to footage and other support materials, and the rationale for making the film in this way at this time.

SHOT TYPES

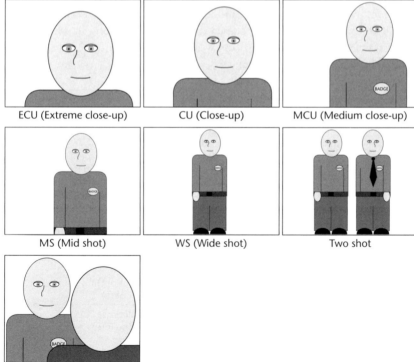

ECU (Extreme close-up)   CU (Close-up)   MCU (Medium close-up)

MS (Mid shot)   WS (Wide shot)   Two shot

OSS (Over-the-shoulder shot)

| Low angle | Eye level | High angle |

Basic Camera Moves

Panning left to right or right to left: the camera moves from side to side with no movement in the vertical plane. This is most effective when using a tripod (loosen the tripod head). Always ensure that you have a clear start and end point so that the pan appears finished.

Tilting: the camera moves up and down with no horizontal movement. Again it is best to use a tripod, and the start and end points are important. If you don't have these fixed it will be difficult to incorporate the shot into your final edit.

Zooming in and out: the focal length of the camera lens moves closer or further away from the subject. The camera itself does not physically move (this would be a tracking shot). It is the focal length that changes. When you zoom in closer to a subject, you will be getting a "tighter" shot. As you zoom out, you will get a "wider" shot. It is not good practice to zoom in or out when someone is speaking. Zooming out may communicate that what the interviewee is saying is not worthy of the audience's attention. Zooming in gives the impression that something important is being said, something to take note of, to sit up and listen. Use the zoom sparingly and wisely.

Following: this is when you are holding the camera, either on your shoulder or under your arm, and you are following someone while walking. You will need to practice this shot: you will need to keep the camera steady so that the shot does not wobble.

The following list is adapted from the entry qualification criteria established by *Skill Set*, the Moving Industry Standards Organisation. You can use this list to ascertain where your key strengths and weakness lie. In which areas do you need practice and/or professional assistance?

Performance criteria	*You must be able to:*
	• Select a camera and/or video recorder appropriate to the task and check it thoroughly before use • Record and monitor audio levels • Select appropriate microphones for the assignment, or make adjustments for the characteristics of the available options • Check camera settings and carry out white balance before proceeding to record video in the appropriate medium and format • Identify and promptly deal with equipment failures • Systematically assess a range of locations for suitability and safety • Where necessary, mitigate problems presented by intrusive and unforeseen noise or visual distractions • Use recording equipment safely, without putting yourself or others at risk or causing damage to property.
	• Keep recording equipment secure at all times • Brief relevant parties on the details of the interviews and the recording requirements • Brief interviewees accurately about the purpose of the assignment, the practicalities and the nature of the video recording process.

- Conduct interviews and record vox pops as appropriate, recognising and responding to unfolding events
- Where applicable, recognise and act on the opportunity to record relevant and effective images, audio and actuality to accompany interviews
- Ensure that sufficient relevant material is recorded for the intended purpose, but be selective, taking into account the amount of original recorded material likely to be used in the final product
- Recognise legal or compliance issues, and seek advice where necessary
- Review the brief in light of the material gathered and judge whether changes in value, treatment or writing are necessary and/or further raw material is required
- Label all video materials accurately in line with established protocols. Save and store them securely
- Maintain comprehensive records of materials, sequences and actuality to support editing and archiving processes
- Where necessary, produce accurate editing instructions to accompany the recorded material
- If appropriate, record a commentary at the location
- Complete the recording of material in line with deadlines
- Transport your material from location back to base using an available/appropriate means of delivery (bearing in mind the confidentiality of the material collected and the platforms for which it is intended).

Background research: identifying and approaching interviewees

The groundwork for audio–visual interviews is broadly similar to that for audio work. Until you develop a reputation for consistency and integrity you are essentially asking interviewees to make a leap of faith. Relationship building and contacts are key. Everyone has to start somewhere, and as noted in Section 4, the innocent abroad can occasionally fare better than a well-known broadcaster. However, you must be upfront. Do not try to hoodwink people into thinking that you are more experienced or more senior than you are; honesty is the only acceptable policy. It makes sense to spend some time researching and getting to know a community before embarking on filming. A combination of openness, genuine curiosity, humility, common sense and manners will go a long way. The most important card that you carry is your reputation; it is much harder to repair than equipment. Once you have established the trust of key individuals in your field you will begin to develop a network of contacts and gatekeepers. In Section 1 we invited you to view things from the perspective of an interviewee. In Nick Broomfield's film *The Leader, the Driver, and the Driver's Wife* (1991) the main focus is access to Eugène Terre'Blanche, founder and leader of the AWB, a South African far right pro–apartheid organisation. Broomfield's efforts are concentrated on Terre'Blanche's driver and, by proxy, his wife. The reflections and interactions of these individuals reveal more about Terre'Blanche's life than could ever be gained from an interview with 'the Leader'. In the end Broomfield and his crew are granted an interview with Terre'Blanche, only to be sent packing after the first question because they had the audacity, as Terre'Blanche put it, to arrive ten minutes late.

This film illustrates a number of points. First, access can be problematic. Your ability to clear the ground, make contacts and read clues are crucial. The better your contacts, the better your access. Second, keep an open mind – interviewees (or information) that at first seems peripheral could become centrally important.

Funding networks and distribution

Filming tends to be more costly than audio work (because of the associated equipment, expertise, software, processing, personnel, permissions, insurance, travel and so on). It is thus likely that you will need to raise sponsorship. The tips offered in Section 3 will help you to approach this issue. As with funding for any interview-based project, it is important to think outside the proverbial box. Your project may inform social history, heritage, minority rights, awareness of diversity, empowerment of the elderly, market research, management, economic forecasting, employee rights and so forth. Without compromising your principles, you may be able to adapt an aspect of your research to suit a sponsor's needs.

Specific questions an interviewee might ask

- Who are you (the filmmaker/researcher)?
- Who are you representing (organisation, online, print, radio, television, advertising or production company)?
- To whom are you are affiliated (company, organisation, union, academic institution)?
- How is your research being funded (public, private, matched funding)?
- What is your film/research about?
- Do you have a pre-ordained 'angle'?
- Who is the main interviewee?
- Who else is participating?
- What is required of other participants?
- How will they be represented (types of shots, supporting material, camera, microphone, lighting, set-up)?
- What outputs have you planned?
- What kind of a consent form will you require?

Interview technique

The skills described in Section 5 are all relevant to audio-visual work. You need simply to adapt them when you are working with a camera. Rather than say 'yes', 'sure', or 'I know', you will learn to nod reassuringly so as not to complicate the edit. To the same end, you might consider pausing briefly before progressing to the next question. We have emphasised throughout the importance of avoiding a prescriptive approach. You must find your own spirit level: once it steadies it will become unique to you, and you will gain confidence in your approach. You can learn a great deal from others in the field, but interviews are intimate encounters and only you can decide what works best on a particular occasion. With audio work you develop a keen ear for a turn of phrase or a 'way of telling'. With camera work you need to develop a further sense of on-screen energy and charisma – this comes with regular camera work and editing experience.

Technical skills

With experience you will develop a hunch for the optimum interview set-up. Likewise you will learn to position microphones to best effect, and you will develop an innate sense of how close you can come to a person without making them feel uncomfortable. You will learn to bounce light off your interviewee's face rather than place a light directly in front of them. For some individuals being filmed is so much water off a duck's back: for others it is at least initially quite daunting. Having mastered the technology, you can focus on putting them at ease. With growing confidence you will come across as relaxed and in control, and your interviewees will follow suit.

Editing

iMovie timeline

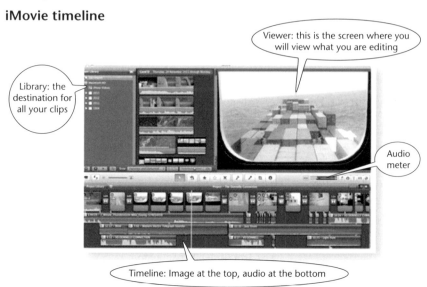

Learning to cut images with voiceovers also improves with practice. Your work might appear clunky at first, but the more familiar you become with the process the more you will learn from existing documentaries. You can also leave from online tutorials. Editing is a creative act, open to all kinds of manipulation, and so it is important to recap periodically on your obligations (to interviewees, funders, sponsors, gatekeepers and so forth). As your editing abilities advance, you will be amazed at the extent to which you can fine tune visual edits and audio sound levels. This cannot be stressed enough. Poor quality sound makes the viewer think they are watching poor quality images, the reverse is very rare. When making a documentary film based on interviews, sound is king.

Errol Morris's film *Fog of War* is an Oscar-winning single-protagonist interview-based film focusing on the US Secretary of Defence Robert McNamara. Editing is used to tremendous effect to build narrative and a compelling story. This is a reminder that a single interview can provide the basis for a full feature-length documentary. Morris encourages the interviewee to look straight at the camera, thereby engaging directly with the audience. He also uses cutaways to vary the scenes and to add context and meaning. Your final edit can be as bold and as creative as you wish, but it should always reflect what your interviewee said both accurately and fairly. You can be controversial, challenging and provocative without misrepresenting.

Edit sound first	Concentrate on what is being said and the order in which it might appear – the beginning, middle and end of your film. Focus on an appropriate and compelling sonic sequence.
Basic cutting	A cut is when a shot changes from one viewpoint or location to another. Cutting may include some or all of the following: • Change of scene • Compression of time • Variation of perspective/viewpoint • Development of an idea.
Establishing the four Ws within a sequence	• Who are the characters? • What is the situation? • Where does it take place? • What is its relevance to the story that I am telling?
Picture and sound edit: *Motivation* *Information* *Composition* *Camera Angle* *Continuity*	There should be a good reason for each edit. Each new shot should provide fresh information. When there is a choice, select the shot that has the best audio, followed by the best composition. Where possible the camera angle should change from one shot to another. Where possible the movement between two shots should be evident (it should not 'jump').
	The ideal cut adheres to all of the above criteria, but in reality we must make the best use of the material and tools available.
In or Out?	If you are unsure about a shot, nine times out of ten it should go. The final edit is all about discarding material that is not essential to the story.

8

STORAGE

Storage is an integral part of the interview process. In the first instance you need to upload, order and catalogue your files. This will enable you to use the material in support of your desired outputs. Long-term storage does not come next; it should be considered before you record your first interview. Your interviewees have a right to know where their account will ultimately reside, so that they can give informed consent, and you have a duty to safeguard our rich oral heritage.

File management – PC

There are two basic options for uploading digital audio files to a computer. The first is to use a connecting USB lead (you will most likely acquire one with your recorder). If you are using a PC you can follow these very basic steps:

- Use the appropriate cable to connect your audio device to your computer (desktop, laptop, tablet etc.)
- Go to 'My Computer'. This is usually on the desktop; otherwise, click Start → My Computer.)
- Your recorder should have appeared here as a USB device
- If you double-click on the icon representing your audio device another icon should appear, this time representing your audio recording. If you have collected a number of recordings you will find the corresponding number of files here
- Assuming that you have previously installed a digital media player you should be able to double-click on the icon representing your audio recording and listen to it (check that your computer speakers are enabled, alternatively insert external headphones).

If you have opted for a recorder with a removable memory card you can remove it and either insert it directly into the computer (assuming there is an appropriate card slot on your machine) or insert it into a memory card reader (these do not generally come with audio recorders and will need to be purchased separately). Once you have connected the memory card (using the reader if necessary) you should go to 'My Computer' as above and check that the recording is intact.

Having uploaded the recording you will need to save a copy to the appropriate folder on your computer.

- Right-click on the icon representing the audio recording
- Follow the drop-down menu and left-click on 'Copy'
- Let go of the cursor/mouse
- Now use your cursor/mouse to open a new folder in which you want to save the file
  ○ You can save directly to a folder such as 'My Documents', but it is best to create an appropriate sub-folder.
    – Open 'My Documents' (if it is not on the desktop, go to 'Start' → 'My Documents') and then right-click
    – Follow the drop-down menu until you come to 'New'
    – Left-click on 'Folder'
    – A new folder will appear and you should have an opportunity to give it an appropriate name, such as 'Audio Recordings'. (Once your interviews begin to stack up it is vitally important that you manage meticulously the naming and numbering of all relevant folders.)
- Once you have opened the appropriate folder in which to store a copy of your audio recording, right-click within it, and following the drop-down menu, left-click on 'Paste'. You should then see the audio file copying to your destination folder.

Before attempting to transfer a live interview it is well worth practicing this process with test recordings.

If you plan to conduct more than a few interviews, you should at the outset establish a clear and comprehensive system for labelling and dating each individual file. To begin, you could number, name and date each individual audio file – for example, '01 JONES, Jack 19 Jan 2013'.

Your 'Interview Files' folder might begin to look something like this:

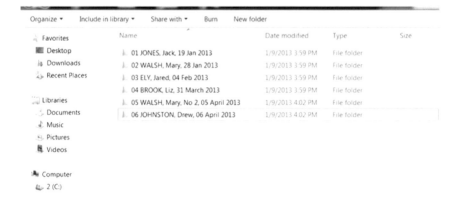

There are no hard-and-fast rules as to how you should store and catalogue your files, but it is advisable to create a separate folder for each interview that you conduct. Within this you can then establish a set number of sub-folders. When you open an individual's interview folder you should then find some or all of the following:

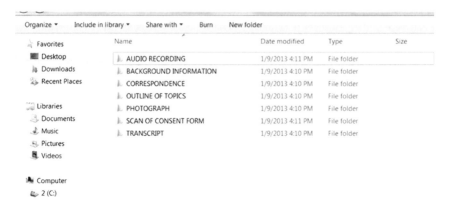

File management – Apple Mac

If you are using an Apple Mac the steps are much the same:

- Use a cable to connect your audio device to your computer (desktop, laptop, tablet etc)
- Open a Finder window (in the Mac dock click on this icon: . Alternatively, on the desktop click on 'File → New Finder Window')
- In the left-hand column of the Finder window, your recorder should appear under the 'Devices' heading

- Click on your device to open its contents in the right-hand column of the Finder window. Your recording should be here
- Again, assuming that you have previously installed a digital media player, you should be able to click on the icon representing your audio recording and listen to it.

If you have opted for a recorder with a removable memory card you can remove this and either insert it directly into the computer or use a memory card reader. Then, as above, open a Finder window and check that the recording is intact.

Having uploaded the recording you will need to save a copy to the appropriate folder on your computer.

- Hold down the 'control' button and left-click on the icon representing the audio recording
- Follow the drop-down menu and left-click on 'Copy [filename]'
- Let go of the cursor/mouse
- Now use your cursor/mouse to open a new folder in which to save the file
  - You can save directly to a folder such as 'Documents', but it is best to create an appropriate sub-folder
    - In the Finder window, click on 'Documents' in the left-hand column
    - At the top of the Mac screen go to 'File → New Folder'
    - A new folder will appear and you should have an opportunity to give it an appropriate name
    - Press 'Enter'
- Double-click on your new folder to open it. Hold down 'Control' and left-click within the folder. Following the drop-down menu, left-click on 'Paste Item'. You should then see the audio file copying to your destination folder.

On an Apple Mac, your 'Interview Files' folder might begin to look something like this:

The contents of your individual interview folders will also look broadly similar on an Apple Mac:

Interview log

In addition to individual interview folders you should create a running log for your interview collection. This will help to facilitate the preservation and long-term viability of your material. Once established, maintaining this catalogue will become routine and it will save you (and future archivists and users) time in the long run. It can be saved electronically in a spreadsheet or table, or in writing. Get into the habit of updating it every time you complete and upload an interview. Each oral archive will have its own system of documenting and cataloguing interviews, but it is always helpful to include the following:

Interviewer Details	Surname	
	Forename	
	Contact details	
	D.o.B.	
Interviewee Details	No.	
	Surname	
	Forename	
	Contact details	
	D.o.B.	
	Role, occupation	
Date of interview		
Location of interview		
Length of interview		
Make and model of recorder		
Recording notes		
Access restrictions		

File checklist

It is also a good idea to keep a checklist to help chart and monitor your files.
For each interview tick as appropriate:

Audio recording ☐

Consent and copyright waiver ☐

Photograph ☐

Outline of topics ☐

Interview notes ☐

Transcript

　Original ☐

　Edited ☐

　Final ☐

Correspondence

　Approach letter ☐

　Thank-you note ☐

　Letter returning script ☐

　Other correspondence/notes ☐

Back-up

Having uploaded and saved a master copy of your audio recordings and all supporting files, you must create a back-up. This is particularly important if you plan to wipe/delete and then re-use your memory card. (This is advisable unless you can afford to purchase a series of memory cards or you only plan to record a small number of interviews). Electronic copies of photographs, consent forms and basic Word documents (including lengthy transcripts) will occupy a relatively small amount of space, but you should be aware that wav files are generally quite large (approximately a gigabyte (GB) per hour of audio). Unless you plan to conduct a very large number of interviews the hard drive of your computer will most likely accommodate the files you need to save, but when selecting an external drive for back-up you will need to calculate how much space you will require based on the total number of interviews you plan to complete (allow approximately 2 GB per interview).

Managing large interview collections

If you plan to conduct more than, say, twenty interviews, you might consider engaging an administrative assistant or – if your budget allows – a project manager. Sourcing and conducting interviews can be all-consuming, leaving little time for administration and processing. If you are under pressure to complete your interviews within a set timeframe you can easily become overwhelmed and may be forced to cut corners in terms of processing and cataloguing your files. If you can, engage someone to assist with:

- Set-up
    - Correspondence
    - Follow up phone calls to arrange interviews
    - Reconciliation of diaries
    - Booking of venues
    - Confirmation of appointments
    - Co-ordination of team of interviewers.

- Processing
    - Uploading of files
    - Retrieving signed hardcopy files (for example, consent forms)
    - Transfer of audio files to transcriber
    - Retrieval of audio files and transcripts from transcriber
    - Light editing
    - Issue of transcript to interviewee with SAE
    - Retrieval of script from interviewee
    - Finalising of script (in line with interviewee's wishes)
    - Maintaining all relevant databases
    - Identifying and closing gaps
    - Reviewing security
    - Assisting with preparations for final deposit at sound archive.

Delegating these vital tasks to an administrator will allow you to concentrate on negotiations with interviewees, the conduct of interviews, the refinement of your matrix, the analysis of interview accounts and the creation of end products. This is not always possible. Interviewing is often akin to waiting for a bus: you linger for half an hour and then three come along at once. Second chances are hard to come by, and so you are inclined to jump when opportunities arise. You should nonetheless try to set aside some time each month to attend to routine administration and to update and manage your files.

WORKING BACKWARDS

One of our earlier research projects drew primarily on documentary sources. A few select interviews were anticipated, as a means of supplementing and correcting existing records. With thirty interviews in hand, the scope and quality of the oral testimonies forced us to backtrack. Rather than a by-product, they constituted a data set of substance and unique character, unquestionably meriting preservation. The accounts varied greatly in quality and range, but there was a common thread that justified their preservation as a whole: each provided a perspective which could not be gleaned from other sources.

Rationalising and upgrading what became a standalone interview collection was cumbersome and time-consuming. Interviewees had to be revisited in person and the terms of collection and deposit revised. (Where the interviewee had since died we had to negotiate with their next of kin.) Recording technologies were adapted and upgraded where possible. The interviews had to be retrospectively numbered and catalogued. Gaps had to be closed and inconsistencies resolved. Biographical notes (which could easily have been compiled at the outset and checked with the interviewee) now had to be written and the entire interview process had to be documented and described.

Tasks that could (and should) have been attended to at the outset took several months to complete, and taught us a very valuable lesson about the need to think ahead before embarking on research interviews.

Processing transcripts

As noted, we often supply interviewees with a copy of their transcript so that they can review it and highlight corrections or redactions. If your interviewee is elderly, the arrival of a seemingly endless succession of typed pages can be overwhelming (a one-to-two hour interview will generate a transcript of around thirty to fifty pages in length). If you can spare the time, it is best to go through the transcript with them and help to highlight any necessary changes. You might also consider increasing the font and spacing if their eyesight is impaired.

Once the interviewee has reviewed the script you can produce an 'edited' or 'agreed' version. This must be clearly marked as such to avoid confusion with the original. The question then arises of what to do with the original voice recording and transcript. Any archivist or historian will urge you to preserve the originals if at all possible. If it contravenes the assurances you have given an interviewee and/or you do not have the resources adequately to safeguard the confidentiality of the original unapproved material, you may have to consider permanently deleting elements of the original. Before embarking on this path you should ask a suitably resourced archive if they would consider holding the original material under embargo. If your interviewee is satisfied with the security protocols in place it might be possible to preserve both the verbatim and the edited transcripts together with the original recording. In thirty (or more) years' time it will be of tremendous value for students – indeed, anyone who is interested in their heritage – to identify the issues that their ancestors deemed sensitive. In many instances these handwritten edits will be more revealing than the original script.

If there is no proportionate and agreed way of preserving the original documents, you should note that it is nowadays quite straightforward to edit a digital recording. For example, Audacity is a popular, free and multilingual audio editor that can be used with Windows, Mac OS X, GNU/Linux and other operating systems. You can use it to record, convert tapes and vinyl into digital recordings or CDs, and edit sound files. *Before embarking on an editing process it is vital that you carefully label and save the original.* You can then create a new copy entitled 'edited audio recording' (or 'edited transcript'). That way you will still have something to fall back on should you accidentally delete the recording whilst editing. (Note that this procedure does have implications for storage, because creating a second copy of your recording will obviously occupy almost double the amount of space on your hard drive.)

Whatever editing programme you decide upon, it is imperative that you study the instructions carefully before commencing (check for online tutorials that will guide you through the process). In the first instance you will need to import your audio file (Audacity can import wav, aiff, au, ircam, mp3 and ocg files). You will then be able to edit your recording as you wish. Depending on the end product you have in mind, you may wish to 'clean up' the recording in order to improve the sound quality, cut out interference (coughing, wheezing, rustling of papers etc.) or add special effects and ambiance. With the right equipment and software there is no end to what you can do with an audio recording, but unless you are adapting your material for use in film or television, it is likely that your main concern will simply be to effect the changes requested by your interviewee (correct, add or delete specified words).

In order to pinpoint a particular section of a recording you must listen to it while observing the graphic representation of the sound on your computer screen. Once you have identified the point at which the relevant section begins and ends you can highlight it with your mouse. You must then play back the section to ensure that you have not selected too much or too little (you can extend or contract the selection as necessary). Using the 'Edit' menu you can then either cut or copy the selection onto a clipboard, just as you would with a Word document. That selection can then be pasted into a new track or deleted. Copying and pasting selections is very useful if you are selecting specific quotes to play as part of a presentation or exhibition. Once you have selected all the relevant quotations you can mix them together in a single track. In Audacity you simply highlight all relevant tracks and then select 'Quick Mix.'

A word of caution regarding the editing of a sound recording: our focus is naturally on what the interviewee has to say and a noisy dishwasher is likely to be an undesirable distraction, but background noise is not always unwelcome. The steady tick of a clock on the mantelpiece, the tweet of a bird on a windowsill, the whistle of a kettle on the stove – all of these can help us more fully to enter into the world of the interviewee. For example, the ticking clock can add a subtle sense of time passing, of the pace of the interviewee's life. This is yet another reason to consider preserving a copy of the original recording before engaging in a pragmatic or present-centred editing process.

Long-term storage

When designing an interview-based project there is a natural tendency to focus on short-term needs. We are often under pressure to meet deadlines of one kind or another and to 'get the job done'. All too often, once an interview has served its immediate purpose the original recording is left to languish in an attic or in the recesses of a poorly-resourced local archive. This is a betrayal of our duty to safeguard original material, and depending on its nature, it may also contravene obligations under data protection legislation. Inattention to long-term storage thus raises ethical, legal and moral issues.

A key challenge is the pace of technological change. In the blink of an eye our chosen medium can be overtaken by new models and software. Analogue recordings (cassettes, CDs and minidiscs) are obsolete without a functioning playback machine complete with all necessary cables and adapters. The log referred to above (including the exact make and model of all recording equipment) will greatly assist archivists and future users. Similarly, it is important to note that a significant amount of video material has become redundant because the playback machines are no longer available. You may well need to encode your videos into newer digital formats, but bear in mind that heavy image compression can seriously erode quality. Take great care to preserve and protect both the original physical tape recordings and the playback machines. Digital codes and file types with which we are currently familiar will also be overtaken in time, and again a log is important.

If time permits, you might also consider creating additional supporting documentation. It will add greatly to your interview collection if, in addition to audio recordings, transcripts, schedules of topics and basic recording details, you can provide an overview of your methodology, biographical thumbnails, copies of your interview notes and any correspondence with interviewees. Annotating your transcripts (translating slang in square brackets and providing notes on key individuals, organisations, events and themes) will contribute meaning and increase ease of use. You may also consider depositing with the interviews copies of any documentary material provided by interviewees (subject to agreement with both the donor and the archive).

Preparing to deposit a collection

We have insisted that the original recording is a precious document that should be preserved in the interest of transparency, falsifiability, integrity and heritage. The best way to ensure the long-term viability of your interview recordings is to deposit them with a suitably resourced sound archive. Begin by listing all the possible depositories in your area. You must then ascertain a) if they accept audio material and b) if they might be interested in taking your recordings. If the answer to both of these questions is 'yes', you should then check to ensure that they have the resources necessary to ensure the long-term preservation of your files. If some of your material is subject to an embargo then you also need to ensure that the archive has the resources necessary to maintain complete confidentiality in processing and storage.

Many local libraries and archives will gladly accept your recordings, but if they are simply consigned to the basement to gather dust, the deposit may ultimately prove futile. This is a particular concern if your recordings are not digitised. In this instance you must identify a sound archive that is capable of storing and converting your original recordings and adapting them in tune with evolving technology.

Digital/Audio-visual repositories

Digitisation has transformed the possibilities for archiving both sound and print material. Many countries now have national digital repositories for historical, social and cultural data. The benefits are many – physical storage space is no longer a constraint, and there is virtually no limit to the volume of material that can be 'taken in'. There are also endless opportunities for linking data and adapting audio and audio-visual material to suit an array of multi-media resources and platforms.

Terms of agreement

Depositing your recordings with a suitable repository should safeguard your material into the future and ensure that your recordings reach a wide audience. At the same time you must ensure that the terms and conditions you agree with an archive match the assurances given to interviewees. As noted, you should ideally confirm the terms of deposit and access before starting to record interviews. This will enable you to name the archive or repository on your consent form and to spell out exactly what will happen to the material in the long term. This is not always possible, and with most research projects there is a certain amount of feeling one's way. It is often only with a clutch of interviews behind us that we turn our thoughts to long-term storage and preservation. In these instances it is necessary to revisit interviewees (or their next of kin if they have passed away) to negotiate the terms of the deposit.

Tariff walls

Although publicly funded archives and repositories rarely charge for access to their holdings, you should establish whether or not the home you select is likely to charge for access to your interviews in the future. This may well be a necessary evil, but your interviewees have a right to know whether or not they (and their relatives) will have to pay to listen to contributions that they freely gave.

Set out below is an example of a simple open-ended clause enabling you to deposit our interviews.

PRESERVATION IN ARCHIVE / REPOSITORY

We/I (name of individual(s)/institution(s)) wish to preserve your interview material by depositing copies at an appropriate archive/repository. Aside from the uses set out above, it will not be released for consultation until (date). By signing this waiver you agree to copies of your interview material being deposited.

Signed   ....

Date   ....

Witnessed by   ....

The waiver authorises you to deposit your interviews in an archive, but bear in mind that sound archives and repositories will also have their own terms and conditions. In order to safeguard the future viability of your recordings (migrating data in line with technological developments etc.), the archive may need you to assign copyright in the recording to them. If your collection is big enough, if it contains confidential information or if it is in any way controversial, there must be a robust agreement. You should appreciate that the depository – while striving to be fair – will look primarily to its own interests. If you have concerns about the terms of the deposit agreement, consult a lawyer. A poor agreement could transfer risk to you and this could prove very expensive.

9

ANALYSIS

If you are collecting recordings on behalf of a third party your final responsibility may be the uploading and cataloguing of your files. If, on the other hand, you plan to use your interviews to support outputs you will need to consider how best to analyse and present your material. The extent to which you dissect and ponder the presentation of your data depends both on the nature of your research and the end product. If your interviews have been designed to capture nodules of information (for example, simple facts, feedback about a specific experience, or details of involvement in an event) you may need simply to tabulate and compare responses.

There is a vast philosophical literature on objectivity and subjectivity and- arising from this – several schools of thought on the interpretation of interview material. Numerous issues – from choice of topic, selection of interviewees, interview structure, interpersonal dynamics, language, and mode of analysis - could be examined. But epistemology need not take over. Taking a neo-empirical approach, one can acknowledge these issues – direct, immediate and general – and, recognising the imperfection of the decision, by-pass them. This is a rational choice to gather imperfect knowledge.

What then are the key points of concern?

Representation

Much can be gleaned from a single interview. If you want to engage in a 'thick' analysis (looking in some detail at form and meaning – issues such the structure of language and narrative, context, performance, distortion, distilling and disremembering) you may not need a large sample. It will also make sense to let the interview flow, with minimal interference and disruption.

On the other hand, if your interviews are designed to inform a broader social or political analysis you will most likely want to capture a cross-section of perspectives and viewpoints.

In Section 4 we discussed a number of strategies for identifying, approaching and accessing interviewees. It is important to remember that the manner in which you select sources will influence the nature of the data you collect. Analysis of interview material often involves the identification of patterns and themes, and as you present those patterns there is often an implication that the interviews are broadly representative of a particular locale, class, group, industry or organisation.

Sampling is usually associated with quantitative interviews – highly standardised accounts that are amenable to statistical analysis. We have demonstrated that qualitative interviews may have a sampling element, albeit restricted statistically. Interviewees can be selected in some kind of balanced fashion, to represent different points of view, age groups, genders, functions, experience and so on. We suggested that these categories can be organised on a grid or matrix that is then subject to periodic review.

The extent to which your sample is representative depends on your strategy. If your group is self-selected (as is often the case with studies of diet, living habits and so forth) you need to acknowledge its limitations. Other possibilities we have cited include drawing on a representative database, or combining personal contacts and subsequent snowballing with a targeted approach (for example, involving advertisements across the relevant media). Subjectivity cannot be eliminated: some interviewees will die before you reach them, and others will decline to be interviewed. A degree of structure will nonetheless help to avoid over-reliance on a narrow range of groups and perspectives.

Falsifiability

The qualitative interview project needs to be particularly cautious in this area. Karl Popper cautioned that a sound theory must have the quality of refutability – no theory can be said to be 'proved', only 'not disproved'. It is all too easy for an unskilled or misguided interviewer to fall into the trap of targeting and capturing information to support a theory. There is also a danger of 'observer bias'. As interviews stack up and patterns begin to emerge, we may begin (almost subconsciously) to hear what we want to hear, and by dint of the questions we pose, solicit information to support our thesis. Careful planning and design (in terms of the selection of interviewees and the interview structure) can help, but the self-awareness, experience and integrity of the researcher are critical. At all times we must maintain the discipline referred to in Section 5, endeavouring to enter fully into the world of the interviewee, leaving both the side and back doors open and always showing willing to amend or adapt our theory in line with the evidence (however inconvenient that may be). A moment's reflection shows how absurd the converse would be.

Reliability

Are there ways of establishing comparative reliability, and what constitutes reliability in these circumstances? Replicability can present a problem for the qualitative method, since no two interviews can ever be the same. However, we may mitigate this in a number of ways. When we make claims and mount an argument we can give others the chance to assess the process that we have followed: we can document our processes (how interviewees were identified, selected and approached), we can preserve an outline of the topics that we covered, and we can provide access to the interviews in sound and/or transcript form.

Memory

While attempts at interdisciplinary examinations of memory have produced little in the way of common ground, there is a general agreement that memory involves a process more complex than the straightforward retrieval of information. We all reshape our memories to make sense of past and present experiences. Maintaining an identity, especially a political one, involves a continuous process of construction and reconstruction. (Articulating a proposition of existential philosophy, Simone de Beauvoir suggested that one is not born, but rather one becomes, a woman. Most theologies similarly emphasise that all human beings are in the process of becoming.)

We must also come to terms with our regrets; otherwise we run the risk of extreme stress. Much has been written about the suppression and filtering of memory. Consciousness itself cannot be supposed to be an open door to the world, as Freud and other thinkers so convincingly argued. Some matters are so painful that we approach them obliquely; we may hide, disguise or even obliterate them (misremembered, repressed and retrieved memories). Even in a long process of psychotherapy or psychoanalysis, some memories may remain wholly or partially inaccessible. To imagine that one can cross more than preliminary thresholds in a research interview would be truly naïve.

As well as subconscious defences and filters, there are more obvious sources of distortion. Our subjects cannot but be influenced by their knowledge of subsequent developments and by a torrent of representations – images, photographs, books, documentaries, films, museum exhibitions and commemorations. Certain vehicles of memory – especially those that are broadcast in film and on television – have particular potency, and some interviewees, through repeated reflection, recitation and polishing, have perfected the art of self-justification.

Scholars have long since established that 'false' memories, silences, evasions, omissions, suppressions and distortions are not necessarily diminishing. What is told in an interview is only part of the story; how and why that information is presented is often equally, if not more, revealing. We do not wish to rehearse here the vast literature on the frameworks of narrative and memory. As we set about analysing and disseminating our findings it is nonetheless important to remember that interview material cannot somehow plug us into the past with unwavering accuracy.

It's the way I tell 'em

What an interviewee tells you can only fully be understood in the context of the encounter – how, when and why it was set up, where and when it took place, by whom, for whom, and for what purpose. Furthermore, the precise nature of the story may change from day to day. As noted, some interviewees' memories may be coloured by an item that they have heard on the morning news or by their present circumstances. (We once conducted an interview with the spouse of a war veteran who spoke in glowing terms about her husband. She approached us a year later to say she wanted to do a follow-up interview, now that she had left him. The facts did not change, but her reflections and her perspective did.)

Knowing me, knowing you

Another obvious variable is the interpersonal dynamics between interviewer and interviewee. We have noted that we are all inclined to see people in social categories and to temper our approach accordingly. The story of a weekend away can be presented in numerous different ways (to a taxi driver, your colleagues, a spouse, children, your best friend, a law enforcement officer or a counsellor). The structure and relative formality of a research interview should minimise frivolity and facetiousness, but the process of 'reading' one another is still an integral part of the interview process.

We have emphasised the importance of language and terminology. When you are reviewing transcripts you can often pinpoint the exact moment at which an interview shifts gear – when the interviewee either relaxes into the encounter, or battens down a number of hatches. This is usually in response to something that the interviewer says. Very few interviewees will call a halt to an interview in response to a word or term employed by an interviewer, but you can often sense a subtle change of temperature.

Choices of vocabulary and terminology raise difficult issues. It is tempting to assume a touch of your interviewee's colouration in the interests of empathy and rapport. This is fine as long as it does not serve to deceive: even if it risks a rebuff, you must disclose all relevant issues which could affect a decision to participate or co-operate. Likewise, in the course of the interview it is best not to stray from the terminology, terms and conditions agreed by your project.

It goes without saying that there is no such thing as the ideal interviewer (or the perfect interview). If you share a similar background with your interviewees (social, political or educational) you may have a ready 'in'. An outsider cannot hope to compete with a ready-made shared cache of local knowledge, connections, trust and understanding. On the other hand, it is sometimes more difficult to explore topics of a sensitive nature with neighbours, colleagues, family or friends, and there may be instances of shared myopia and the like. If you are publicly associated with a cause of one kind or another you may find that some interviewees skew their accounts accordingly, telling you what they think you want to hear or leaving out bits that they deem unpalatable to you. The important point is to reflect on the interviewer-interviewee relationship and to acknowledge the ways in which this might have influenced the nature of the evidence collected.

Coding

By their very nature, oral testimonies are inchoate. The level of recorded detail is an undoubted bonus, but it can be difficult to structure and render into readable prose. It is very easy to become overwhelmed by data. Deriving meaning from hundreds of hours of recordings and/or pages of transcript is a major challenge. While qualitative interviews do not offer the kind of statistical possibilities we associate with standardised questionnaire-driven interviews, it is possible to code findings.

One way to begin to make sense of your accounts is to assign tags or labels identifying those fragments that have a general character. You might begin with an open coding system and then proceed backwards and forwards through refined categories. (For example, 'corporal punishment' and 'playground games' might come under the umbrella of 'Education', while 'sibling rivalry' and 'divorce' might come under 'Family'.) Once you have begun to link your data codes you may wish to introduce some quantitative analysis (you can use either a good word-processing package or a software programme like Ethnograph, NUD.IST, askSAM, ETHNO or InfoSelect). This might help you to compare the responses of men and women, young and old and other categories. (If you plan to publish your transcripts online you can use hyperlinks to enable users to move between linked codes, themes and events.)

Together with systematic sampling, coding can help to safeguard against leaning on interviewees, opinions or quotes with which you happen to agree. A limitation of this approach is that it can by its nature flatten the data, stripping away key contextual detail such as the specific question posed, the form of the story, the manner of the delivery, performance and so forth. However, it can be helpful in revealing patterns, consensus, dissent, omissions, contradictions and ambiguities.

Interpretation

Coding is simply one way of ordering your interview data. The next stage is interpretation and analysis. In Section 1 we set out a selection of possible outputs (book, article, film, radio/television documentary, audio-visual exhibition, report etc.). Here, the selection of evidence is critically important. Coding or thematic analysis should help to expose the full range of perspectives and opinions contained within your data set, but what quotes do you select in support of an analysis? Interviewees' views are often complex, contradictory and shifting – but your prose or script must have clarity and focus.

In order to make presentations as lively and engaging as possible there is a compelling temptation to fly to the most colourful quotations – and to the most talented and articulate story-tellers (those with a wicked sense of humour, a wonderful turn of phrase and a string of telling anecdotes). This brings us back to the issue of representation. How do we account for the not-so-colourful majority? Television and radio programmes are notoriously selective: hours of recorded information must be condensed into minutes of airtime, and the finished piece must be lively, engaging and to the point. We recently adapted ten audio-visual interviews to support a short film on education. A script of four thousand words (supported by soundtracks, cutaways and contemporary footage) was distilled from more than eighty thousand words. Less than five per cent of the interview material was represented in the final output. This is a fairly standard rule of thumb.

In presenting quotations there is a temptation to clip, clean and clarify. We have noted that every transcription, no matter how faithful, is a translation, and that you should resist any temptation to distort or falsify what the interviewee said. However, presentation can still alter meaning in subtle and unintended ways. Splicing and joining quotes, eliminating questions, grammatical errors and repetition can all serve to alter meaning. What then of the interviewee? To what extent have they been left behind? Does their story still ring true? Has the nature of 'informed' consent changed in the new light of your analysis?

Where's my story?

We have given a good deal of thought to interviewees' fears about 'going public' and of being quoted out of context. Some will want to remain anonymous (if so, you need to check whether or not they want to be mentioned in a general list of contributors). It is important also to remember that some individuals, having given an interview, fully expect to have their account publicised. There are many reasons for omitting an interviewee's evidence in your final analysis or presentation. It may be that they simply did not address the topics that you finally settled on, that they made libellous, defamatory, or unsubstantiated claims that were likely to do more harm than good, or that their account was generally vague, ill-directed and incoherent. It is therefore important to explain that you may not be able to draw on all accounts in the final product. If the omission of an interviewee's account is likely to be noted and to give offence, try to forewarn them. You have a duty of care to your interviewees that extends well beyond the interview, and the last thing you want is for some poor soul to turn up at an exhibition or to purchase a book and anxiously leaf through it, only to feel disappointed and let down when they discover that their story does not feature. Far from being empowered, they may well feel dejected, diminished and used.

'That's not what I said'

If you select quotes to support an analysis with which your interviewee disagrees, they may get upset and may even feel exploited. Katherine Borland offers a telling illustration of the challenge of reconciling interpretative rights. She interviewed her grandmother and then drew on the account to support a feminist analysis. Her grandmother responded as follows:

> Not being, myself, a feminist, the 'female struggle' as such never bothered me in my life. It never occurred to me. I never thought of my *position* at all in this sense. I've always felt that I had a fine childhood. It seems, now, that I must have had a remarkable one [...] So your interpretation of the story as a female struggle for autonomy within a hostile male environment is entirely YOUR interpretation. You've read into the story what you wished to – what pleases YOU. That it was never – by any wildest stretch of the imagination – the concern of the originator of the story makes such an interpretation a definite and complete distortion, and in this respect I question its authenticity. The story is no longer MY story at all. The skeleton remains, but it has become your story. Right? How far is it permissible to go, in the name of folklore, and still be honest in respect of the original narrative?[1]

With hindsight Borland felt that she should have arranged a follow-up meeting with her grandmother to discuss her interpretation. She feels that by extending the 'conversation' in this way, researchers might be able more sensitively to negotiate issues of interpretative authority.[2]

Reflecting on how she and her grandmother managed so completely to misunderstand each other, Borland notes that the fieldwork exchange has a tendency to downplay differences: both investigator and source seek to find common ground from which to proceed to the work of recording.[3] This presents something of a conundrum. The interview relationship is built on trust. It is also thrives on empathy and rapport, which in turn give way to a degree of conviviality and social ease. Without this the encounter would be scarcely bearable for either party. However, once you take the account away, the power dynamics shift. Regardless of how clearly your objectives and projected outputs have been stated, the interviewee may subsequently feel used or misunderstood.

Some interviewers consult with the interviewee at every stage of the process. In some cases the primary motivation for conducting the interview is to empower the interviewee (for example, during reminiscence therapy or community confidence-building). In these instances the interviewee will most likely be involved in any analysis or presentation of their material, and the fear of being quoted out of context is unlikely to arise.

Contested history

The example set out above relates to the interpretation of an individual account, but researchers commonly weave together extracts from a range of interviews. They may be interested in identifying commonalities and differences across the range. All of this makes for interesting academic analysis, but yet again it multiplies the risk of an interviewee – or members of a particular community – crying 'That's not what I said'. There are no easy answers to this. Unless you are focusing on just one or two individuals, you most likely will not have time to revisit your interviewees and negotiate an agreed interpretation of the accounts collected. In divided communities – or in the aftermath of a controversial event such as an accident, a boycott, a strike, an atrocity or a riot – there is often little consensus, and it may be impossible to present an analysis that doesn't offend someone's sense of self or community.

You must therefore arrive at a compromise that addresses your ethical, legal and moral obligations to the interviewee on the one hand, and your right to interpret the material on the other. If you are set on applying a particular type of analysis (for example, feminist, post-colonial, Lacanian) it seems only fair to forewarn your interviewees. It may not be feasible to afford them the right to influence your analysis, but it will enable you to make an informed decision about the likely upset to individual or community relations and to decide if the advantages (for example, raising awareness, ultimately increasing tolerance) outweigh the disadvantages.

We have counselled that interviewers should be prepared to leave the side and back doors open. This denotes a willingness to depart from planned questions and to be taken in new directions by your interviewee. This sometimes jars with the principle of informed consent, since it is only when the available evidence has been assembled and reviewed that the appropriate mode of analysis can take shape.

We have generally offered a degree of shared authority. This involves not only affording interviewees the right to review their account, but also letting them see any direct quotations – in context – prior to publication. Most researchers simply will not have the time and resources to offer this service, and in keeping with your completion obligations, you should never raise expectations by offering an assurance that you cannot deliver on.

In the vast majority of cases your analysis will not present a problem. Thinking you to be a reasonable person, most interviewees will respect your desire and your right to interpret their accounts as you see fit. They will acknowledge that it is rarely possible to arrive at conclusions that satisfy all interviewees – especially if you sought out a deliberately diverse range of opinions. They may actually be pleased to know that their account informed a rigorous and interesting scholarly analysis – whether or not they happen to agree with your conclusions. The alternative – a safe, inoffensive and anodyne analysis – may irritate interviewees and readers alike.

Sanctity of sources

There are strongly-held views on almost every detail of the interview process – about whether to state formalities at the start of a recording, whether to refer to a schedule of topics and so forth. In our experience a degree of flexibility is essential. Each interview project – and each individual interview – must be assessed on its own merits. Within the lifetime of a single project the local or political climate can change considerably, and policies and procedures must be adapted accordingly.

There are nonetheless some basic rules of thumb from which scholars should not deviate:

- Respect the sanctity of the original recording. If at all possible, ensure that it is preserved and made accessible. This will enable others to assess your processes and selection and to draw on the material to arrive at alternative conclusions. You may subsequently be challenged; this is your safeguard.
- Never systematically or deliberately distort the evidence. (This includes ignoring pieces of information or entire accounts that do not fit neatly with your emerging thesis.)
- Within your field, seek out a broad range of perspectives and views.
- Remain vigilant to fresh angles and voices and seek to capture these where possible.
- Be in constant and questioning dialogue with yourself.
- Interrogate oral evidence in much the same way that you would any other type of source. Consider and document motivation, consistency, possible bias, omissions, errors and authenticity.
- Remember that conclusions follow evidence, rather than the other way around: bear Procrustes in mind!
- Consult other sources as appropriate. (The strength and validity of most scholarly and professional analysis rests on the skilful integration of a wide range of sources.)
- Consider the particular strengths and weaknesses of oral evidence and the ways in which these colour the data: the pros and cons of hindsight, interviewer-interviewee dynamics, the fallibility and distortions of memory.
- Thoroughly document processes: the manner in which interviewees are selected and approached, interview protocols and procedures, ethical and legal frameworks, interview structure and content, transcription and editing guidelines, style of citation etc.
- Do not share or publish any aspect of an individual's account until they have confirmed in writing that you may do so.

The extended open-ended interview has many elements of objectivity. It clearly cannot be entirely or even substantially without intent and structure, but it can let the interviewee speak, set out issues, establish facts and create emphasis.

All of these provide opportunities for probing and sideways movement. No knowledge can be complete.

In qualitative interviews we are looking for facts, certainly, but also for interpretations of facts and recollections (which may not be accurate – but that is also of interest). We look for perceptions, ambiguities, feelings, judgements, and justifications.

While we would claim humane and critical rather than scientific status for our qualitative methodology, Popper's axiom provides guidance. It points to a necessary self-awareness on the part of the researcher – a systematic examination of a range of possibilities, a willingness to seek out material which challenges as well as confirms, humility in the face of the fragility of one's evidence, and open-mindedness at all times.

Objectivity always has a human, humane, limited dimension, but in that sense it is complete, since it deals with limited humanity. And so we can proceed with confidence and energy, knowing that this methodology – with all its imperfections – can access data not available by other means and obtain insights which, alone, or in combination with other sources, can be of immense importance.

Notes

1 Katherine Borland, 'That's Not What I Said': Interpretive Conflict in Oral Narrative Research. In Sherna Berger Gluck and Daphne Patai (eds), *Women's Words: The Feminist Practice of Oral History*, London and New York, Routledge, 1991, pp. 69–70.
2 *Ibid.*, p.73.
3 *Ibid.*, p.72.

10
POSSIBILITIES

We have emphasised throughout that interviews – and the skills necessary to conduct them – are applicable to a wide range of professional, vocational and everyday activities. We have also underlined the importance of working backwards from both long-term storage needs and projected outputs.

Modern technology has transformed the dissemination possibilities for audio and audio-visual material. We are in the midst of a digital revolution: it unfolds in wonderful and sometimes worrying ways, but there can be no doubt that it is now the predominant, ever-expanding and evolving mode of communication. Interview recordings increasingly migrate from civic to cyber space, and platforms multiply on a seemingly daily basis.

Once your interviewee has approved their account and transferred in writing any copyright in the recording to you, you are free to use the material to any lawful end stipulated on the consent form.

Functional interviews

If your interviews are designed to inform a specific output (a report of a tribunal or committee of enquiry, recruitment, an appraisal or disciplinary procedure, a medical evaluation, consumer feedback, an official account), your employer or organisation will almost certainly have well-established guidelines for presentation and compliance.

For those working beyond these confines the creative scope will be much greater. In this short concluding section we recap on the type of output you might envisage, and cite some of the productions and collections that have impressed us most.

Exhibitions and archive collections

Major sound archives function both as generators and magnets for interviews. The British Sound Archive holds one of the largest collections in the world (over one million discs and several thousand tapes). Notable projects include The Century Speaks: Millenium Oral History Project and National Life Stories. North American repositories include the Columbia Center for Oral History (home to more than eight thousand oral and visual interviews), the Smithsonian Institution Archives in Washington DC, and the Foreign Affairs Oral History Collection of the Association for Diplomatic Studies and Training at the Library of Congress. In many instances folklore and oral history collections are housed under one roof. The National Library of Australia Oral History Collection, for example, holds interviews about both social history and prominent Australians, together with folklore material.

Not surprisingly, some of the most striking collections focus on war and atrocity (for example, World Wars I and II, the Holocaust, Vietnam, the 1994 Rwandan genocide and 9/11). The International Coalition of Historic Site Museums of Conscience was founded in 1999 by a number of bodies including Memoria Abierta in Argentina, the Gulag Museum in Russia, the Slave House in Senegal and the Lower East Side Tenement Museum in the United States. Interviews are used alongside art installations, documents and other exhibits to intensify awareness and sharpen experience, provoke public dialogue and community organisation and promote human rights. The Coalition currently includes seventeen sites of conscience and a network of seventeen hundred initiatives in ninety different countries.

One of the great attractions of the interview is its ability to capture a diverse range of perspectives – all kinds of victims, perpetrators, observers and onlookers. One thinks here of the work of the Austrian journalist and historian Gita Sereni, who was best known for her interviews with controversial figures such as Mary Bell (who was convicted in 1968 of killing two children when she herself was a child), Franz Stangl (commandant of Treblinka) and Albert Speer (an architect who was a major figure of the Third Reich).

Social change

Accounts from those hitherto hidden from history are especially important. The following topics stand out: women's history, underrepresented racial and ethnic groups (for example, native Americans, Aborigines, various black communities) and emigration. The collection and exhibition of such material has often a direct social and political purpose. For example, at Toynbee Hall in London the Trace project explored the history of youth culture in the East End. This intergenerational work involved reminiscence interviews with elderly citizens at the Older People's Day Care centre, and helped to break down barriers between young and old. Likewise, London's Eastside Community Heritage uses interviews both to preserve local heritage and to build partnerships with schools, families and adult learners, thereby raising awareness about social ills such as racism.

Reminiscence therapy

Life story interviews have been employed as a form of direct therapy for elderly citizens, particularly those suffering from dementia and Alzheimer's disease. Recordings can be used alongside music, photographs and memorabilia to create memory books and exhibitions.

Dealing with the past

There is a manifest need to address residual legacy and memory issues in post-conflict societies. Well known mechanisms include the South African Truth and Reconciliation Commission (established on the basis of the 1995 Promotion of National Unity and Reconciliation Act and designed to help deal with the legacy of apartheid), the Swiss Peace Foundation's Dealing With the Past programme, and An Oral History Approach to Balkan Memories on War, Peace and Justice (established by the Hague Institute for Social Justice). The African Oral History Archive (sponsored by the Ichikowitz Family Foundation) uses interviews to create educational packages, broadcast documentaries, eBooks, feature films, art collections, web portals and public seminars to fulfil their belief that 'redemption is found through remembering'. In Northern Ireland important work is being done by peace and reconciliation groups and by organisations such as Healing Through Remembering, but there is yet little agreement about how to deal with the past.

Everyday life

Cataclysmic and horrific events yield powerful and gripping testimony, but some of the most interesting and thought-provoking collections focus on the banality of everyday life. Here we have in mind the world-renowned Mass Observation project housed at the University of Sussex.

History of professions, vocations and organisations

Interviews have been used to capture the history of various professions, vocations, organisations and ways of life. The Archives of American Art, for example, contain an important series of interviews documenting the history of visual arts in North America. In many countries important work has been done on the history of the legal and medical professions. Political elites have naturally attracted much attention (one thinks of Allan Nevin's work at Columbia University). The history of agriculture calls to mind George Ewart Evans' interviews in rural Suffolk. The Bullock Texas State History Museum houses an impressive photographic and oral history collection focusing on contemporary women who work the land as ranchers, farmers and cowgirls. Sporting and cultural organisations such as the Irish Gaelic Athletic Association have also engaged in extensive interview collection.

Local, family and community research

Local archives and museums are home to the ever-expanding range of family history interviews. Although the focus may be confined to one's own family, do not underestimate the historical value of the material collected. Likewise, although long-term preservation is not the primary concern of anthropologists, sociologists and political scientists, the raw material created in the course of their research may well be treasured by future generations.

Online exhibitions

Many projects (such as Civic Voices, a joint initiative of Civics Mosaic and the Democracy Memory Bank) prioritise worldwide access to recordings. The interactive possibilities are endless. The Sisterhood and After: the Women's Liberation Oral History Project (Centre for Life History and Life Writing Research, University of Sussex) is a typical example. In addition to an interview archive they are producing academic outputs and interactive online resources, integrating audio material with a range of relevant primary and secondary sources.

Broadcasters are increasingly working to digitise their own archival collections. This has facilitated the publication of valuable online resources: we think here of BBC exhibitions such as *Chronicle* and *A State Apart* and RTÉ's *Century Ireland*. Digital repositories can also function as a central hub for privately held material. One major limitation is that they do not accept analogue recordings but, in countries like Ireland where there is as yet no national sound archive, they at least offer some facility for the preservation and dissemination of audio recordings.

Schools and colleges

Schools have provided a powerful vehicle for the collection of interviews, both with and by pupils. The Irish Schools' Folklore Scheme (1937–38) encouraged schoolchildren to document folklore and local history. Some one hundred thousand children were involved in the collection of oral and written material, resulting in more than half a million manuscript pages. This type of material can be adapted to great effect to suit younger visitors. For example, the National Film and Sound Archive of Australia developed a Pause and Play feature which invited children to explore the 'family tree' of film and sound.

Colleges and universities have also developed important interview collections. The Pacific Lutheran University at Tacoma, Washington, has the Scandinavian Immigrant Experience; Harvard houses the Iranian Oral History Project; The

Avraham Harman Institute of Contemporary Jewry at the Hebrew University of Jerusalem holds fifteen hundred oral testimonies from child survivors of the Holocaust; and the Oral History Centre at Mary Immaculate College, Limerick, Ireland houses many valuable collections.

Academic outputs

The range of books and articles that have drawn on interviews – whether exclusively or in combination with other sources – is too vast to review here. Some authors that have particularly influenced us include Ronald Fraser, Tony Parker, Allesandro Portelli, Studs Terkel, Paul Thompson and Alistair Thomson.

Interactive seminars

Academic outputs are no longer confined to hardcopy. We have noted that interviews are increasingly exhibited online. They can also provide the basis for live witness seminars (as exemplified by the work of the History of Modern Biomedicine Research Group at Queen Mary, University of London).

Literary adaptations

Perhaps the most powerful interview-related outputs are those that reflect both the cadence and the content of oral testimony. We think here of theatrical productions such as London Road (which drew on interviews concerning an appalling series of murders of sex workers in Ipswich). In some cases topics are so sensitive that the page can barely hold the testimony. Adapting a model developed by Teya Sepinuck in the United States and Poland in the late Eighties, the Northern Ireland Theatre of Witness company gives voice to those who have not been heard in public before. Life stories are performed by the witnesses, putting a public face on issues of hidden human suffering.

Films and documentaries

In Section 7 we drew attention to possibilities for documentary and film work, and noted that nowadays there is no end to what can be achieved on a shoestring budget. Recent docudramas that draw on interviews to great effect have included Channel 4's *Everyday* and the BBC's *The Village*. Casting our minds back to the Sixties, a timeless example of the intersection of interview and art can be found in Ewan MacColl's radio ballads. These one-hour ballads consisted of recordings made with members of the public, script and songs by MacColl, musical arrangements by Peggy Seeger, production and editing by Charles Parker, and musical participation as necessary. These intricate tapestries of speech, sound and music transformed radio documentaries and opened our ears to a revolution in sound.

CREDO

Looking back at our manual, our hints on how to do and (we know we are finger-wagging) lists of instructions; and considering all the details that lie between the covers of this guide; we worry that the enjoyment and discovery of interviewing, its unique possibilities, its inspiring and transformative qualities, may have become overlaid with a Pompeian ash-cloud of worthy facts and warnings. So here are our final words. We can all do it: some of us with inventive magic and dazzling flair; most adequately, with occasional passages of inspiration; some struggling, but nevertheless able to claim the midwife's glory.

Words on a clay block, stone, papyrus or page have moved us for millennia, whether they are of belief, love, adventure or pity, or any other interval of that limitless spectrum into which we vicariously enter. Within not much more than a century the recorded word and word and image have emerged and a filter has been removed. The sound (and visual) interview at its very best brings us within the living shadow, the space, footsteps and breath of another human. Pitiful or repellant, full of grandeur, stiff with dignity, warm with humour or transfixative in compassion, all have become so much more directly available to us. Whether it is a narrative, entire or crafted, the subtle labour of pointillism, or flashes that light some long-lost or hidden landscape, the interview captures, keeps and transmits. We have here tried to show how. To do it, you must know why.

Our distant ancestors told tales, to the sound of music, in the rapture of movement, in front of paintings and carvings, with light and warmth. We inherited this impulse and will never shed it, or the need for such magic. Technology has placed in our hands new means to tell, to collect and to pass on. It is a worthy, timeless and constructive activity.

Whatever takes you to the interviewer's humble encounter, remember you walk along a path trodden by our kind since times scarcely to be imagined and emerging from that transformative moment, many times achieved and lost, when observation became reflection and that became knowledge.

INDEX